曹保明
CAO BAOMING

著名文化学家；
中国文学艺术联合委员会全国委员 ；
吉林省文联副主席；
吉林省民协主席；
中国民间文艺家协会副主席。

Renowned cultural scientist;
National Committee Member of the China Art and Literary Committee Association;
Vice Chairman of the Jilin Province Federation of Literary and Art Circles;
Chairman of the Jilin Province Folk Literature and Art Association;
Vice Chairman of the China Folk Literature and Art Association.

边 缘
BIAN YUAN

自然地理摄影师；
中国摄影家协会会员；
美国摄影家学会会员；
英国皇家摄影学会会员；
荣获中国国家林业局森林文化奖；
荣获WWF世界自然基金会自然奖；
荣获中国摄影艺术最高奖金像奖作品奖。

Nature and Landscape Photographer;
Member of the China Photographers Association;
Member of the American Photographers Association;
Member of the British Royal Photographic Society;
Winner of the Forest Culture Award of the China State Forestry Administration;
Winner of the Nature Award of the World Wildlife Fund;
Winner of the Golden Medal Award, the highest honor in the field of photography in China.

中国冰雪文化遗产经典读本

Classic Reader of The Ice and Snow Heritage of China

冰湖腾鱼

Fishing on the Ice

查 干 湖 最 后 的 渔 猎 部 落

The Last Fishing Tribe on the Chagan Lake

边缘 著

By Bian Yuan

撰文 曹保明　摄影 边 缘

NATIONAL GEOGRAPHIC
美国国家地理

摄影 / 闫来锁
Photograph by / Yan Laisuo

冰湖腾鱼

CONTENTS目录

永远的查干湖

THE ETERNAL CHAGAN LAKE

写在《冰湖腾鱼》前边的话

An Introduction to *Fishing on the Ice*

撰文 / 高材林

By / Gao Cailin

在人类的生活中，其实我们每一个人每一天都在寻找，寻找一个越来越感觉到能吸引你、能留住你的地方，这个地方往往是人真实生活的地方，但又超越了现实本身。这里往往是生活本身留住了一些生动的东西，或者是山，或者是水；或者是村落，或者是人家；哪怕仅仅是一座老院落，一座老房子，一棵老树，那是一些忍不住让人去思考的东西，这里才是作为有生命的人去苦苦寻觅的地方。

In human life, each and every one of us is in search of something, looking for a place that increasingly draws us in and keeps us from leaving. It is often a place where people lead real lives, and yet which transcends reality. It is here that life itself retains something vivid, perhaps mountains and waters, villages and people, or even something as simple as an old courtyard, an old house, an old tree. These are the things that make you think, and such are the places that people who are truly alive strive to find.

英国著名文化人类学家查理斯·多尔森（Charles Dorsen）认为，社会不能不发展，自然不能不变化，而在所有的发展与变化中，那些“留住了传统”并在进程中能使传统与自然和社会“很好衔接”的地方就是人类进步的典范。以世界文化学家的理论和结论去权衡，中国吉林省的查干湖冬季渔猎就具有这样的性质和身份。在这里，它具备了人类所有自然文化与传统文化很好融合的条件和能力，它完成了这些实践，并很好地保留了传统留给人类的成果。

Charles Dorsen, the renowned British cultural anthropologist, argues that society cannot but develop and nature cannot but change. However, amidst all the developments and changes, those places that "retain traditions" and, in the course of progress, are able to link nature and traditions with society, serve as paradigms of human progress. Gauged by this standard, the winter fishing at Chagan Lake in Jilin Province of China can be seen as such a place. It has all the conditions and abilities for the ideal integration of natural culture and traditional culture, and has well preserved the fruits of human traditions.

人类的传统，是指人类在生存的语言、行为和心理上的一种综合体现，这种体现必须是这个地方具有自己久远的历史、清晰的传承、活态的存在和鲜明的地域特色，查干湖冬捕渔猎就是这样一个典型。在这里，这块土地上的久远历史都很好地保留在了它的渔猎生活之中，它没有从历史和自然中把自己剥离出去，而是主动地靠近自然、保护自然，让自己成为自然中的存在，这在当今社会普遍讲发展而又不知如何递进的进程中非常重要，它以自己的实践留住了自然，也留住了自己。与别的地域截然不同的是，查干湖的渔猎留住了属于它自己的完整的渔猎传统。在这里，我们会清晰地看到久远的文化基因的过渡层次，以人为代表的传承，在人的血缘关系和社会以及职业关系上，都清清楚楚地体现着，甚至，我们可以倾听到、看得到、触摸到、感受到这种文化，也可以与之对话，并参与到传承的因素中去。我们真真切切地呼吸到这块土地上的清新美妙的传统生存气息。在这里，近百岁的渔猎文化传承者携着他的诸多 80 岁、70 岁、60 岁、50 岁、40 岁以至更年轻的传承者，都留在这块土地上。这里保留了一种传统文化的前所未有的完整性和清晰性。走进查干湖，你会发觉自己走进了优秀传统文化的缜密结构之中，这种结构是永远不会失掉的。

Human tradition refers to the comprehensive embodiment of human beings' language, behavior and psychology for survival. This embodiment requires that a place have a long history of its own, clear inheritance, active existence and distinctive regional characteristics. The winter fishing on Chagan Lake is such an example. Here, the long history of the land is well preserved in its fishing life. It has not torn itself away from history and nature; instead, it has taken the initiative to come close to nature and protect nature, and let itself be an existence in nature, which is all too important in today's society, where talk of development is everywhere, with little knowledge of how to manage the process. The people of Chagan Lake have preserved the place and surrounding nature by doing what they do. What makes the place utterly different from other regions is that it has preserved its fishing tradition in its entirety. Here, we can clearly see how the cultural DNA has been passed down through the ages and gone through transitions. The heritage is clearly embodied in blood relations as well as social and occupational relations. What is more, we can even hear, see, touch and feel the culture. We can enter a dialogue with it and become part of the legacy. We breathe the refreshing air of a traditional culture that is well and alive. Here, the hundred-year-old preserver of the fishing culture guides and teaches inheritors who are eighty, seventy, sixty, fifty, forty or even younger, while living together with them on this land--a land that has preserved a traditional culture with unprecedented integrity and clarity. Once you enter the world of Chagan Lake, you will find yourself within the finely meshed structure of a splendid traditional culture that will never be lost.

衡量所有优秀文化的标准只有生活本身。在查干湖，我们可以明确地感受到它与社会、与生活、与自然、与文化、与历史的关系，特别是它与现实社会的关系，人们在这里才实实在在地感受到查干湖渔猎生活已与今天的社会生活多么的不可分割，那已形成了一种生活链，它是活着的传统，它是活态的文化基地，它是现实人们所需要的一种生动的生存方式。同时，人们又清楚地感受到，这里具有属于自己的鲜明的地域特色，这是使它一跃而成为人类文化遗产的重要条件和身份。在生活中，其实任何一块土地、一个地域，都有自己的鲜明特色，但是在认同这个特色、保护这个特色、挖掘这个特色、传承这个特色上，别的地方很难超越这里。

The standard for measuring all good cultures is life itself. At Chagan Lake, we can clearly feel its relationships with society, life, nature, culture and history, especially its relationship with the real world. Here, one truly feels that the Chagan Lake fishing life is inseparable from life in today's society, with which it has formed a chain of life. It is a living tradition; it is a living cultural base; it is a vivid way of life that people need. At the same time, one will also clearly feel that it has distinct regional characteristics of its own. They constitute the critical conditions and identity which have made the place a cultural heritage site of China. In fact, any piece of land, any region, has its own distinct characteristics. However, in terms of identifying with these characteristics, protecting them, exploring them and passing them down, no place has done better than Chagan Lake.

一个地方，它的真实能力不在于如何昭示、宣传，它应该做的恰恰是如何去认识它自己。一个不能很好认识自己的地域，就没有未来，很真实地认识自己、思考自己，才能完善自己，才能根据自己的本土存在去认真地审视自己与人类的自然、历史与文化的关系，也才能找到自己。查干湖最大的成功是很好地找到了自己，也就找到了他人。它立足于本土，也才找到了世界，进入到人类文化的层次。

A place’s true value lies not in how it displays or promotes itself, but in how well it knows itself. No place that fails to understand itself has any future. Only by truly understanding itself and reflecting on itself can it improve itself, and, based on its existence on the land, further to examine itself in relation to nature, history and cultures, ultimately discovering its true self. Chagan Nur's greatest success lies in having found itself, which has allowed it to find others. Only by remaining rooted in its own land has it found the world, and become a shared human cultural heritage.

查干湖渔猎文化的所有存在，完完全全地得益于留住了自然的原始背景优势，并在保护这个重要自然基因的进程中，一刻也未停止地保住更加重要的生存传统，那就是作为三大人文要素的语言、行为和心理。这种保持和生存，使得查干湖得天独厚地占据了人类社会向文明发展过渡的前沿高度，它没有让自己离开人类社会发展的文明前沿，因此它具备了冲向人类文化顶点高度的能力和品质。

The Chagan Lake fishing culture owes its existence entirely to having retained its natural environment, through the process of which the people tirelessly preserved the traditions linked to their survival, namely the three major cultural elements: language, behavior and psychology. This has allowed the culture of Chagan Lake to remain at the forefront of human society's development towards civilization, endowing it with the ability to reach the height of human culture.

若干年以来，人类社会处于匆忙的转换期与转型期，欧洲的工业革命发展到工业文明的今天，恰恰与中国的工业化、城镇化异曲同工。在中国社会与人类文化发展的全球化背景之中，人们在苦苦地寻找失落的曾经创造过人类思想与文化辉煌的遗产，可是，都不知不觉地被发展的理念轻易地忽视掉了。查干湖的存在，一下子突显出它的珍贵和重要了，很少有例子在当今可以说明传统在一个地域和一个民族中的价值意义，查干湖恰恰以自己的真实、朴实、生动的身份和完整的传统文化结构向人类做出自己的答案，这里才是人类理想的去处，是人类千百年来苦苦寻觅又接续要去构建的地方，它的存在，是全人类的一个奇迹。

For many years now, human society has been in a fast-paced period of transition and transformation. The progression from the industrial revolution to an industrialized civilization in Europe is mirrored by China's industrialization and urbanization. Against the cultural background of globalization and the social and human development in China, people are struggling to find what has been lost, the legacy that once created glorious human thoughts and cultures, which, nevertheless, has been unwittingly overlooked and replaced by newly-discovered ideas. Chagan Lake's existence highlights how precious and significant this legacy is. Today, no other place better exemplifies the importance of tradition to a region and a people than Chagan Lake, and it has done so with an identity that is authentic, down-to-earth and vivid and a traditional cultural structure that remains intact. It is the ideal place to be for humans, one that we have sought long and hard for and will continue to build. Its existence is a miracle for all mankind.

如今，全球都在变暖。人类渴望到达一个美妙的冰雪世界，冰雪铸就的庭院楼阁，处处雪树冰花，仿佛这些只能在安徒生童话和普希金听外婆讲的传说中才有。其实，查干湖就是这样的一个地方。在这里有白雪铺就的原野，有冰湖凝成的晶莹的冰原，那些五彩缤纷的冰与雪的文化都是它自己的内涵。在这里，美丽梦幻的冰雪不再是一个单纯的背景和空间，它有自己的述说，那一串一串的故事、传说以及传说和故事中的人物，许许多多的冰雪记忆，都可以活生生地与你对话，这里在亲切地拉着你的手，让你能够融进故事和传说。梦幻其实已是生活本身。冰雪佳境，晶莹剔透，冰走马轮，霜结人脸，鱼腾冰湖，汉唐飞天，苍狼踏冰，人畜与共，一处完整的自然与社会完美融合，被人类很好保留和发展出来的生命生存佳境，奉献给了人类文化遗产宝库。查干湖，其实是自己保住了自己，自己留住了自己。

Today, the world is getting warmer. Humans long for a wonderful world of ice and snow, where courtyards and pavilions made of ice and snow are everywhere, surrounded by snow trees and ice flowers. It might seem that all these can only exist in Andersen’s fairy tales and the legends that Pushkin's grandmother told him. In fact, Chagan Lake is just such a place. Here, there are snow-covered wilderness and ice sheets formed by crystalline ice lakes, which are given meaning by the colorful culture of ice and snow. Here, the dreamlike ice-scape is no longer a simple background and space. It has its own narratives. The string of stories, legends, and characters in the legends and stories, and all those memories hidden in the ice and snow, talk to you as if they are alive. This place holds your hand cordially so that you can immerse yourself in the stories and legends. In fact, here life itself is a dream. This wonderful land of ice and snow, of crystalline clearness, of horse-drawn wagons on ice, of frost-covered faces, of fish leaping out of the lake, of the Han and Tang flying Apsaras, of wolves crossing the ice, of men and beasts living side by side — all this shows a perfectly preserved harmony between nature and humans, contributing to the treasure trove of human cultural heritage. In so doing, Chagan Lake has preserved itself, all by itself.

高材林
2016 年 10 月
Gao Cailin
October 2016

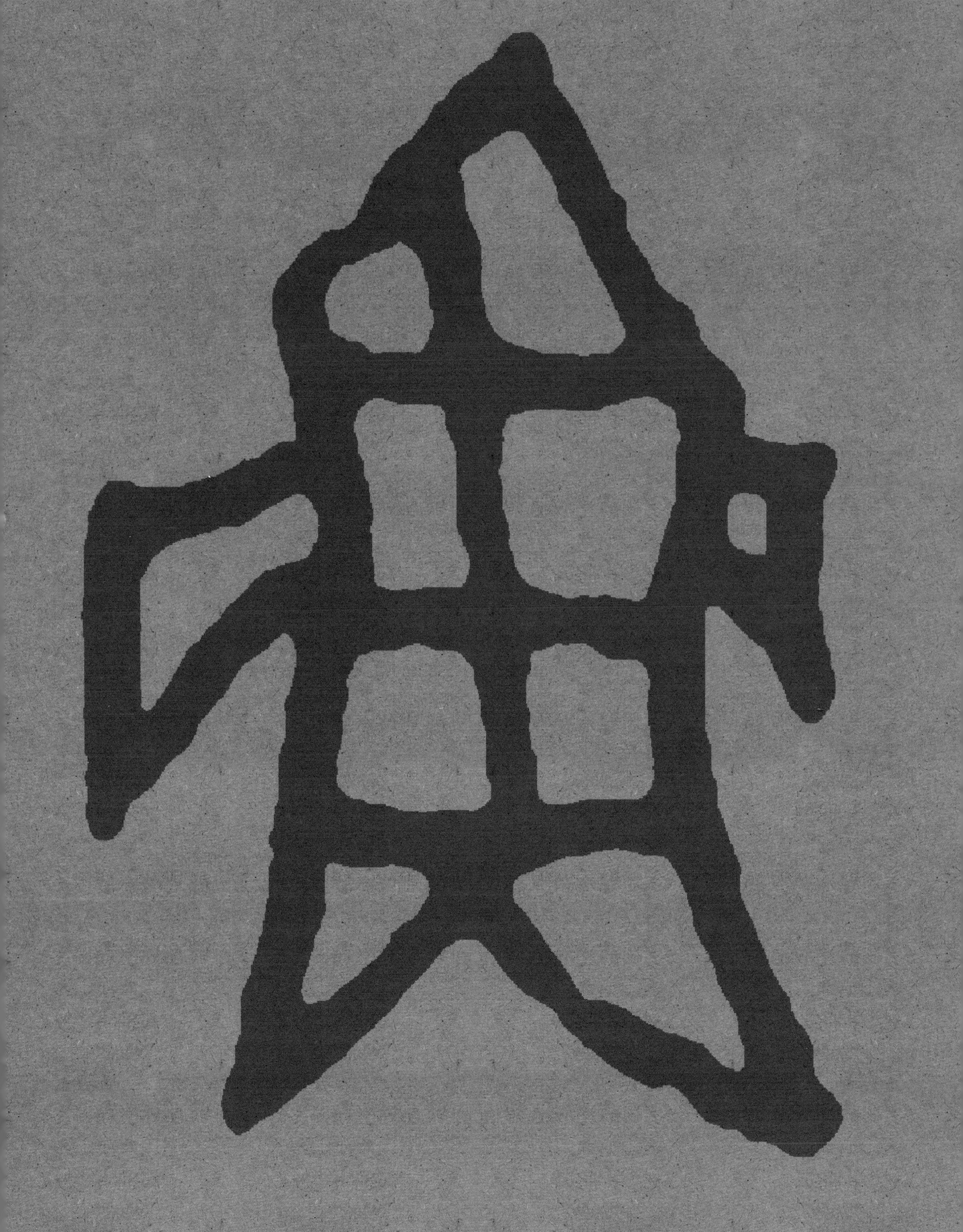

Legends of the Snow Field

雪野传奇

在东北，从深秋到初冬，一切江河湖泊都封冻了。

历史上，

北方交通十分不便，一到冬季，

许多封冻的大江大河便成了爬犁道，

如果渔民们在江上凿冰捕鱼，

往往会使爬犁和大车不便通行。

北方人心是善良的，冬天，

他们不在大车和爬犁行走的冰道上打冰眼，

于是便选择在泡沼湖泊一类的水域上凿冰捕鱼，

这样查干淖尔就成了北方冬天最具特色的天然捕鱼场。

In Northeast China, all rivers and lakes are frozen from late autumn to early winter.

Historically, transportation in Northern China has always been hard.

In winter,

many frozen rivers become sledge roads.

If fishermen chisel the ice on the rivers to fish,

this makes it hard for sledges and carts to travel.

But the northerners are kindhearted,

and they do not cut ice holes on any of the ice roads along which carts and sledges travel in winter.

Instead they cut holes on frozen ponds, moors or lakes to fish.

Thus, Chagan Nur became a most unique natural fishing ground in China's northern winters.

霜凝大地多苦寒，雪刮冰湖又一年，风云开处网旗展，荒原马啸鱼腾欢。在地球的北部，每年，当寒风吹落了树上的叶子，当严霜杀枯了草原，当北风裹着茫茫大雪来到查干淖尔，一个古老的传说就回荡在人间……

The frost-covered land is filled with bitter cold, and the snow falls on the ice lake year after year. Flags unfurl in the wind, and horses neigh while fishes dance in the wilderness. In the north of the earth, every year, when the cold wind blows leaves from the trees, when the frost withers the grassland, when the snow wrapped in the north wind sweeps across Chagan Nur, an ancient legend circulates among the people...

相传，在远古时候，人间非常穷苦，人们饿得头晕眼花。百姓就期盼，如果老天能降下来白面该多好啊！终于有一天，天空真的飘起了白面，那纷纷扬扬的白面，就像今天的大雪一样，人间再也不挨饿了。

According to legend, in ancient times, people were so poor and so hungry that they prayed for god to rain wheat flour down from the heavens. At last, one day, wheat flour really started to drift down from the sky, just like snow. And the people were never hungry again.

人们乐啊！跳哇！从此过上了丰衣足食的日子。

How happy the people were as they leapt with joy! From then on the people lived in want of nothing.

可是有一天，这样的好日子被一个人破坏了。有一户人家，由于天上降下了白面，他们觉得再也不用劳作了，再也不用种地了，就开始懒惰起来。

However, this good life was destroyed one day. One family, thinking that they did not have to work or farm anymore since the flour came from the sky, became lazy.

人哪，咋能这样？

They should have known better.

有一天，天上的神仙想，自从天上降下白面，人间该是不挨饿了，他们生活得怎么样了呢？神仙就决定来到人间巡察看一看。这一天，神仙来到了民间，事情也凑巧，神仙正好来到了懒媳妇这家人家的门前。神仙把自己打扮成一个穷乞丐。

One day, it occurred to the god that the people should not be hungry any more since he had sent wheat flour down to them. He wondered how they were doing. So he decided to come to the mortal world for an inspection. And so it happened that on the day the god descended to earth, disguised as a beggar, he came to the house where the family had grown lazy and was met by the lazy wife.

风，将白雪涂抹在晶莹的冰原上，谁碰倒了丰满的鲜奶桶，让优质乳油绘出了荒原严冬？
Wind has applied snowy paint on the glistening ice sheets. Who upset the milk bucket and covered the winter wilderness with the finest cream?

摄影 / 闫来锁
Photograph by / Yan Laisuo

神仙走到那家门口，说："有吃的给我一口吧？"
媳妇说："你是谁？"
神仙说："我是要饭的。"
媳妇说："去去去……，我们都饿得没有饭吃！"
神仙听后吃了一惊，问："天上不是下白面了么？"
媳妇说："那还不得自己动手做么？多累呀，如果直接掉馅饼该多好啊！"
神仙一看，她旁边有六个孩子饿得哇哇哭。

The god went to the door and begged, "Give me a bite to eat, please!"
"Who are you?"asked the wife.
"I'm a beggar."
The wife said: "Go away... we are hungry, and there is no food!"
Astonished, the god asked, "Isn't it true that you have flour from the sky?"
The wife said: "But still we must make our own food. How tiring! If only we could have meat pies fall from the sky!"
The god looked around and saw her six children crying from hunger.

神仙气坏了，他回到天上，把在人间看到的事情一五一十地向玉皇大帝禀报了一遍，之后说："咳，人哪，太不知理啦，太不知足啦！"

玉皇一听，立刻下令，从此再不降面，把面变成雪。于是从此，天上就每年飘下纷纷扬扬的大雪了。

这虽然是一个民间千古流传的故事，可是，这则传说教育了人，启迪了人，从此人懂得了珍惜资源的道理。

The god was furious. After returning to heaven he reported what he saw in the mortal world to the Jade Emperor, commenting: "These mortals, how ignorant and insatiable!"

Upon hearing this, the Jade Emperor immediately commanded that the flour be changed into snow. After that, snow drifted down every year.

Although this is a folk legend, it has taught and enlightened people to treasure resources.

北方冬季飘飞的大雪虽然不是白面，却是自然给予我们的最好的资源，你不用，人依然会受穷。你看冬季的冰雪，可以把大地变成坦途，各种大车可以在上面自由行走，于是人们发明了爬犁，这种创意是北方民族的智慧，历代北方民族已普遍使用。而且，人们选择冰雪来做建筑材料，什么院墙啊，仓库啊，都可以用冰雪来完成。冬季还把食物用冰雪埋起来，成了天然的大冰箱。甚至灯啊，盏哪，都可以用冰、用雪来制作。至于堆雪人、蘸冰糖葫芦，那更是北方人生活的冰雪趣话了。这时候，人开始意识到，其实冰雪是北方独有的重要的自然资源、历史资源和生活资源，它不次于天上降下的“白面”呀。就这样，人开始精心设计这个资源，使用这个资源，开发这个资源，利用这个资源并得益于这个资源，于是，一个巨大的冰雪资源宝库开启了……

The drifting snow in the northern winter is not flour, but it is the best resource endowed to us by nature, and people must make the best use of it or be poor. You see, the winter snow and ice turn the earth into smooth roads where a variety of carts can travel freely. Then people invented the sledge, which is widely used by northern peoples and demonstrates their ingenuity. Moreover, people choose to use snow and ice as building materials for courtyard walls and warehouses. In winter, people use snow and ice as a large natural refrigerator under which food is stored. People even make lamps with ice and snow. As for snowmen and frozen sugar-coated haws, they represent the fun side of the northern life. Now people have begun to realize that, in fact, snow and ice are important natural, cultural and life resources, unique to the northern part of the country. It is not inferior to the “flour” from the sky. Thus, people have begun to carefully design, use, develop and benefit from this resource, as though opening the gates to an immense treasure trove in the ice and snow...

摄影 / 闫来锁

Photograph by / Yan Laisuo

巨冰起雪原，大雪落查干

Huge blocks of ice stand on the snow fields, while heavy snow falls on Chagan Lake.

松花江和嫩江交汇处的松原是一处独特的地方，当年孙中山先生曾在《建国方略》中称此地为“东镇”，是想在这个水草旺盛、湖泊群集的地方建东北最大的城镇。三江交汇把这块土地和草原滋润得无比肥沃和富饶，星罗棋布的泡沼湖泊散布在这里的土地上。这儿可以称之为一个多湖泡之地，仅在前郭尔罗斯地域内就有大小湖泊27处之多，而其中一个独特的名字“查干湖”不但是这儿最大的湖泊，同时它又是中国十大淡水湖之一。

Songyuan, located at the confluence of the Songhua River and the Nenjiang River, is a unique place. Dr. Sun Yat-sen referred to it as "East Town" in the "General Plan for Founding the Country", meaning to build this place of abundant grasslands and lakes into the largest town in Northeast China. The convergence of three rivers has made the land extremely fertile and bountiful, with potholes and lakes scattered throughout. It can well be called the land of lakes and potholes. There are as many as 27 large and small lakes in the Qianguoerluosi Region alone. One of the lakes, named Chagan Lake, is not only the largest lake here but also one of the top ten freshwater lakes in China.

查干湖蒙语为查干淖尔，意为“白色圣洁的湖泊”。它地处吉林省松原市前郭尔罗斯蒙古族自治县境内，北纬45° 09′ —45° 30′ ，东经124° 03′ —124° 34′ 的位置上。查干淖尔是今天的称呼，据《辽史》记载，在宋辽时，它被称之为“大水泊”或“大鱼泊”。据《辽史》记载：“鸭子河在大水泊之东，黄龙府之西，是鸭雁生育之处。大水泊周三百里。”到了明代，这片大水泊被称为“拜布尔察罕大泊”（也称“白马儿大泊”）。它是发源于大兴安岭得福特勒罕山北麓的霍林河末端的堰塞湖泊，靠四季的雨雪，汇各处的水源而形成。由于查干淖尔古时的自然状况保存得好，这里的一切生灵都得到了世界的关注。这里湖中的鱼完全是靠水中的浮游动植物为生，于是被人们称为天然的营养品，有极高的养生价值，从远古时起就引起了人们的注意。

The lake is known as Chagan Nur in Mongolian, meaning "white holy lake". It is located in Qianguoerluosi Mongolian Autonomous County in Songyuan, Jilin Province, or, more precisely, at latitude 45° 09'-30' N and longitude 124° 03'-34' E. Chagan Nur is its present name. According to the *History of Liao,* in the Song and Liao dynasties, it was called "Big Water Pond" or "Big Fish Pond". The *History of Liao* records: "The Duck River to the east of the Big Water Pond and west of the Yellow Dragon Prefecture is a place where ducks and geese multiply. The Big Water Pond is three hundred *li* in area."

In the Ming Dynasty, this Big Water Pond was known as "Paibuerchahan Big Pond" (also known as "White Horse Pond"). It is a barrier lake at the end of the Huolin River, which originates from the north of the Defutelehan Mountain of the Greater Hinggan Mountains. The lake water comes from the rain and snow through the seasons as well as the convergence of several rivers and streams. Thanks to the well-preserved natural conditions of Chagan Nur since ancient times, the creatures here have long attracted the world's attention. The fish here, which feed entirely on the lake's plankton, are seen as natural nutrients with high health values and have been prized since ancient times.

在历史久远的岁月中，人类保护了自然，又使得自己依赖自然并得到了生存。这是北方民族的一种生存习惯，也是一种生存能力。而其实，他们是把包括查干淖尔在内的这一片土地很好地保护了下来。

那时，包括松花江、嫩江在内的诸多条江河上都开始了渔猎生活，查干淖尔也有了夏秋冬季的捕鱼活动。由于这个湖泊生长着独特的自然植物，水中昆虫繁多，鱼儿吃水中的小虫和湖边的草籽，构成了独特的肉质。这儿的风向也奇怪，有时东南风突转西北风，于是刚刚顺向的草籽便会大片的倒向水中，成为鱼儿的美食。

摄影 / 张军
Photograph by / Zhang Jun

In the long flow of history, human beings have protected nature and in turn survived by relying on nature. For the northern peoples, this was not only a way of life, but a survival skill. And in so doing, they have perfectly preserved the land that they live on, including Chagan Nur.

At that time, fishing had begun along a great many rivers, including the Songhua River and the Nenjiang River, and Chagan Nur was also beginning to see fishing in summer, autumn and winter. Unique plants grow around the lake, and insects thrive in the water. The fish feed on the insects

as well as the grass seeds, which contributes to the unique texture of their meat. The capricious winds here also help. Sometimes a southeaster turns to a northwester all of a sudden, causing the grass to bend towards the lake and making the grass seeds easy food for the fish.

而妙音寺和青山头一带地势偏平，生长着荷花、芦苇、菱角、藻类植物，这是鱼儿喜欢吃的，诸多的大鱼秋夏喜欢在这一带活动。鱼儿有了自然良好的生存环境，查干淖尔就成了它们生存的最佳之地。据有关资料统计，仅在查干淖尔内就有各种鱼类68种之多，其中以胖头鱼、鲤鱼、鲫鱼、麻鲢鱼、鳡条鱼、嘎牙子鱼和大白鱼最为著名，真可谓“三花五罗十八子”样样都有，而查干淖尔捕鱼最典型最辉煌的时候就是它的冬捕，即冬季捕鱼。

On the flatlands in the Miaoyin Temple and Qingshantou areas grow lotuses, reeds, water chestnuts and algae, all of which are foods that the fish feed on, and a lot of large

fish can be found here in summer and fall. With such an ideal natural environment, Chagan Nur has become a magnet for fish. According to statistics, there are as many as 68 kinds of fish in Chagan Nur alone. Among them, the best known are the bighead carp, common carp, crucian carp, silver carp, yellowcheek, yellowhead catfish and top mouth culter.The Chagan Nur is thus a veritable smorgasbord of fish species, and the most glorious season

摄影 / 闫来锁
Photograph by / Yan Laisuo

冰原打开了晶莹之门，人走进了独特的地域
The ice fields have opened their crystalline gates, inviting people into a unique realm.

for fishing there is winter.

在东北，从深秋到初冬，一切江河湖泊都封冻了。

历史上，北方交通十分不便，一到冬季，许多封冻的大江大河便成了爬犁道，如果渔民们在江上凿冰捕鱼，往往会使爬犁和大车不便通行。北方人心是善良的，冬天，他们不在大车和爬犁行走的冰道上打冰眼，于是便选择在泡沼湖泊一类的水域上凿冰捕鱼，这样查干淖尔就成了北方冬天最具特色的天然捕鱼场。

In Northeast China, all rivers and lakes are frozen from late autumn to early winter.

Historically, transportation in Northern China has always been hard. In winter, many frozen rivers become sledge roads. If fishermen chisel the ice on the rivers to fish, this makes it hard for sledges and carts to travel. But the northerners are kindhearted, and they do not cut ice holes on any of the ice roads along which carts and sledges travel in winter. Instead they cut holes on frozen ponds, moors or lakes to fish. Thus, Chagan Nur became a most unique natural fishing ground in China's northern winters.

冬捕与平时捕鱼活动不同的是，这是一项集体活动，不是一个人能独立完成的，这需要诸多人的配合，并调动这儿的诸多民族一块参加的一项活动。冬捕就是面对严酷的大自然，去凿冰捕鱼。当地人有个习俗，查干淖尔冬捕时，谁不去冰上见识一下，谁就不是“汉子”。这是对男人体魄、能力的一个衡量。在东北，谁没去查干淖尔打过鱼，谁甚至就找不上媳妇。为了冬捕，各行作坊都开工作业，木匠打爬犁，铁匠打马掌，车匠扣大车，皮匠做皮袄，鞋铺做靰鞡，编匠编渔具，麻绳铺打绳织网，割苇的人也忙着编鱼囤子……

Winter fishing differs from fishing in other seasons in that it is a collective activity; no one can do it alone. It is an activity that requires the cooperation of many people and mobilizes many ethnic groups. Winter fishing means braving the elements to fish in winter by cutting holes in the ice. In local custom, during the winter fishing season, whoever does not go out on the ice to experience it for himself is not a “real man”. It is a measure of a man’s strength and ability. In Northeast China, no man can find a wife if he has never gone fishing on Chagan Nur. In preparation of winter fishing, all the workshops get busy: Carpenters make sledges; blacksmiths forge horseshoes; cart makers build carts; cobblers make leather coats; shoe shops make shoes lined with *wula* sedge; weavers make fishing gears; hemp rope makers weave ropes; and reed cutters are busy preparing fish snares...

整个查干淖尔，一片忙碌。

冬季捕鱼又使各民族之间，人与人之间得以充分交流。由于要组织渔业队，打工的小股子、网户达，捕鱼人和把头，各种手艺人，还有鱼店的掌柜和老客，各种大车店和旅店，都有了一种交融和联系。查干淖尔冬捕，起到了促进社会的发展和文明进步的重要作用。甚至在冬捕的日子里，动物也得到了重视。马要顶一个“股”到冰上的捕鱼场“拉马轮子”；狗要看网房子；牛要拉鱼、运鱼。冬季的捕鱼活动，使人和动物亲近了，使人和自然得到了实实在在的融合。

只见花开树，不见鸟争春
The trees are blossoming, but where are the spring birds?

The whole Chagan Nur bustles with acitivity.

The winter fishing brings different ethnic groups and communities together. The organization of fishing teams means cooperation and communication among part-time workers, fishing households, fishermen, fishing masters, a variety of craftsmen, fish shop owners, frequent customers, a variety of cart taverns and hotels, etc. The Chagan Nur winter fishing plays an important role in promoting social development and progress. Animals gain new importance in the winter fishing season. Horses pull the winch on the fishing ground; dogs keep guard of the net sheds; and cattle help pull the fishing nets and transport fish. The winter fishing activities bring people and animals, men and nature, closer together.

一切文化和精神在冬捕的日子里得到了全面展示和传承。查干淖尔冬捕是人类生存成果的一次大的、全面的、辉煌的展示和普及。人的品德、人的生存能力、人的精神面貌，都在这种壮丽的活动中充分地释放出来。

这种从春夏就开始准备了的活动，使人们憋足了劲儿，要把在冰层下长了一夏一秋的鲜美鱼儿捕捞上来，于是使查干淖尔冬捕活动形成了自己独特的民俗……

冰封大地，当厚厚的白雪覆盖在茫茫的嫩科尔沁草原上，当老北风呼啸着日夜吹刮的时候，查干淖尔壮丽的冬捕便开始了。

摄影 / 刘玉忱
Photograph by / Liu Yuchen

湿地腾金浪，又到鱼丰时

The wetland is surging with golden waves, another season for harvesting fish is coming.

During winter fishing, all the cultural and spiritual heritage of Chagan Nur is on full display. The Chagan Nur winter fishing is a grand, comprehensive and splendid demonstration of human survival. Through this activity, human character, the ability to survive and the human spirit are released, completely unbridled.

This activity, the preparations for which kick off in spring and summer, releases people's pent-up desire to catch the fresh and delicious fish under the ice, which have been fattening up all through summer and autumn. And it is this activity, the winter fishing, that forms the unique customs of Chagan Nur.

When the land is frozen, when the vast Horqin Grassland is covered with thick snow, when the north wind is whistling day and night, the spectacular Chagan Nur winter fishing begins.

这时候，土地在颤动，马儿在嘶叫，人们在呐喊。那是黑土北方的人们一种抑制不住的热情，在心底升腾。

他们戴上狗皮帽子，穿上老羊皮袄走向冰原。那是一种回归，是一种原色的生存味道，是一种原始古老图腾的复活与复苏。

在地球上，古人类生存的文化形态至今仍能让人直接去体验和感受这种原色的地方如今已为数不多了，可以说是查干淖尔独有的。

进入查干淖尔冬捕，有一种走进远逝的楼兰古地之感，又好似来到秘鲁印地安人古老的生存部落，你会感受到大自然在平凡地接纳你，又在生动地拥抱你。

摄影 / 包文军
Photograph by / Bao Wenjun

部落院落，生态家园之一
A courtyard in the tribal village.

是的，这儿是目前世界上唯一的也是最后一处被自然和人类完整保存下来的传统渔猎文化部落。这个传统的冬季渔猎活动，如今时时被模仿，却从来未被超越。因为它在用自己的故事，述说着自己的冰雪传奇。

And when it does, the land trembles, horses neigh, and people shout. It is the people who live on the black soil of the north boiling over with irrepressible enthusiasm.

They step onto the ice, wearing dog-skin hats and sheepskin coats. It is a return to a primal form of survival, a resurrection of an ancient and primitive totem.

On earth now there are hardly any cultures of ancient human existence left that still allow people to directly experience the more primal world, and Chagan Nur is unique among them.

Encountering winter fishing at Chagan Nur, one feels as though one has stepped into the ancient kingdom of Loulan, or arrived at a tribal settlement of the Peruvian Indians. Here, one feels welcomed and embraced by nature.

Indeed, this is the world's only and last traditional fishing tribe to have been preserved by nature and humans. It is often imitated, but never surpassed, for it has its own stories to tell, the legends written in ice and snow.

摄影 / 包文军
Photograph by / Bao Wenjun

摄影 / 包文军
Photograph by / Bao Wenjun

部落院落，生态家园之二
A courtyard in the tribal village.

Spiritual Blessings

心灵祈福

祭师来到供桌前端起一碗酒走到敖包旁，

用蒙语诵祭湖词：

啊，长生天，先祖之灵；

庇护众生，求昌盛，求繁荣。

查干湖，天父的神镜；

查干湖，地母的眼睛——

啊，歌天唱地查玛舞，鼓乐齐鸣诵经声。

举灯为心台日月，满湖金银庆丰登。

一祭万世不老的天父！

再祭赐予我们生命的地母！

祭祀万灵的湖神，让湖神保佑查干湖连年有余、永世昌盛！

The priest comes to the sacrificial table, raises a bowl of liquor, walks to the *aobao*, and chants a Mongolian prayer in worship of the lake:

Ah, Eternal Heaven, and Ancestral Spirits,
Shelter all beings, let us thrive and prosper.
Chagan Lake, the holy mirror of our Heavenly Father,
Chagan Lake, the eye of our Earth Mother —
Ah, in honor of Heaven and Earth we sing and dance the Charma,
we play music and chant prayers.
Hoist the lanterns as our hearts to call forth the sun and the moon,
Let the lake reflect gold and silver to celebrate a bumper harvest.
First we worship our eternal Heavenly Father!
Second we worship our life-giving Earth Mother!
Then we worship the almighty Lake God;
May the Lake God bless Chagan Lake with year after year
of good harvest and prosperity forever!

摄影 / 闫来锁 心花怒放的查干淖尔

Photograph by / Yan Laisuo Prayer flags flutter near Chagan Nur.

如果说，吉林是一个自然资源无比丰富多样，蕴藏量非常丰厚的地方的话，那么冰雪资源应该是吉林省最具特色的资源之一。远古时期，查干湖的先民就懂得使用冰雪去进行生产和生活实践了，那是因为这种资源最普遍地存在于自然中。冬季，当第一场雪飘落北方，冰雪资源便来到了人间。可是，使用冰雪，人们的心中要有一个明确的遵循，那就是人类千百年的生存习俗的传承。

If Jilin Province is a place with extremely rich and diverse natural resources, then snow and ice are among its most unique resources. The ancient dwellers of Chagan Lake knew how to use ice and snow for production and living needs, because this was the resource most commonly found in their natural environment. This resource arrives in winter, when the first snow falls in the north. However, when making use of ice and snow, people must keep one principle in mind, and that is the preservation of a way of life and customs that have been passed down through thousands of years.

查干淖尔真正的渔猎活动始于13000年前的青山头人。据考古记载，在青山头发现古人使用的网坠、网锤、鱼钩、渔叉等，还有渤海和夫余国时期进行渔猎活动的工具等。据《辽史》记载：每年冬月，冰封大地，辽帝都要率领群臣、嫔妃来塔虎城(始建于辽，原名长春州)，在嫩江、松花江交汇处的查干淖尔湖面上搭起帐篷，命人在湖面上周围十里范围内凿冰下网围鱼，使之不得逃出，然后用数匹马拉绞盘，将毛网聚合到冰口取鱼。钩鱼时，在冰面上搭起帐篷，凿开四个冰眼，中间的冰眼凿透用以钩鱼，外围的不凿透用以观察。鱼到时，观察人告知皇帝，由皇帝亲手钩鱼，第一条鱼谓之“头鱼”，以胖头鱼居多，用以烹调，来款待文武百官以及各地首领和各国使节，称之为“头鱼宴”……等冰雪融化后，野鸭、大雁、天鹅等从南而归，辽帝则开始架鹰鹘捕捉天鹅，晨出暮归，从事弋猎。第一次猎得天鹅，皇帝要设“头鹅宴”大宴群臣以

示庆贺，并邀请千里之内的各女真部落酋长用以安抚……每年，辽帝都要在冰帐内举行头鱼宴、头鹅宴，这是辽帝每年“春捺钵”中的重要政治活动之一。

Real fishing activities in Chagan Nur began with the Qingshantou people 13000 years ago. In archaeological records, net weights, net hammers, fishhooks, fishing forks and other tools used by the ancients have been found at Qingshantou, and other fishing and hunting tools dating from the Bohai and Fuyu kingdoms have also been unearthed. According to the *History of Liao*, each winter, when the ground was frozen, the emperor of Liao (a dynasty founded by an ethnic minority called the Khitan) would lead his ministers and consorts to Tahu Town (Changchun Prefecture in the Liao Dynasty). The emperor would have tents put up by the Chagan Nur at the confluence of the Nenjiang River and the Songhua River, where he ordered his men to chisel the ice and cast a net into the lake around a ten *li* radius so that no fish could escape. Then, horses were used to turn the winch to pull the net up to the ice hole, where the fish could be caught. When it was time to hook up the fish, four "eyes" were chiseled in the ice under the tent, with the middle eye cutting through the bottom of the ice for hooking fish and the surrounding ones used for observation. When the fish emerged, the spotter alerted the emperor, who would personally hook the fish. The first fish thus caught was called the "head fish", usually a bighead carp, and it was used for the "Head Fish Banquet" to treat civil officials, military officers, local leaders and envoys from other countries. When the snow and ice melted and the wild ducks, geese, swans and other birds returned from the south, the Liao emperor began to hunt for swans. From morning to evening the emperor was thus employed, aided by the gyrfalcon. After catching the first swan, the emperor hosted the celebratory "Head Swan Banquet" for court officials and invited Jurchen tribal chiefs from within a thousand *li* as a measure of appeasement. Each year, the Liao emperor would host the Head Fish Banquet and the Head Swan Banquet in a tent over the ice. It was one of the Liao emperor's important political activities at the annual "Spring *Nabo*".

啊，长生天，请来引领你的子孙穿越千年盛典
Ah, Eternal Heaven, guide your descendants in this endeavor passed down through centuries.

摄影 / 闫来锁
Photograph by / Yan Laisuo

让夙愿走进自然与生命的空间
The fishing master leads the fishermen in prayer at the net awakening ceremony.

捺钵，契丹语，是“行在”“行宫之意”，指辽帝出行临时所在地。《辽史·营卫志》载，“辽国尽有大漠，浸包长城之境，因宜为治。秋冬违寒，春夏避暑，随水草就畋渔，岁以为常。”契丹族四时迁徙，故捺钵分为“四时捺钵”，即“春水”“夏凉”“秋山”“坐冬”。辽代契丹族的四时捺钵的产生，不是偶然的，是有其历史背景的。在中国历史发展过程中，10世纪唐帝国瓦解，形成了以长城为界的两种不同社会性质和两种不同文化的存在。长城以南气候温和，居民多为汉民族，人烟稠密，长久以来，人们就已经养牛种地，过着男耕女织的生活，形成了以农耕为主的农耕文化；长城以北，气候寒冷，人口稀少，一直靠游牧狩猎为生，人们在生产劳动中把自己锻炼得体力强健能耐风寒，形成了以游牧为主的草原游牧文化。那时，在北方广袤无垠大地上居住在辽河上游牧区的契丹族，生活方式是以游牧、农耕、渔猎为主，自然形成了其特有的四时捺钵。

Nabo is the Khitan term for "traveling palace", which refers to the seasonal camps of the Liao emperor. The "Records of Camp Guards" in the *History of Liao* contains this passage: "The Kingdom of Liao consisted of vast deserts surrounding the Great Wall area, and the people adapted accordingly. They stayed away from the cold in autumn and winter and escaped the heat in spring and summer, going where the water and grass took them to hunt and fish; thus they lived year-round." As the people of Liao moved around as the seasons shifted, there came to exist four *nabos*, namely, "spring water", "summer cool", "autumn mountain" and "winter stay". The *nabo* system did not come about by chance, but arose from a specific historical background. As China's history unfolded and the Tang dynasty collapsed in the 10th century, it resulted in the existence of two different kinds of societies and cultures, divided by the Great Wall. To the south of the Great Wall lived mostly ethnic Han Chinese; the climate was mild and the land was densely populated. People there had long raised cattle and cultivated crops, living a life of men farming and women weaving, forming an agrarian culture. The regions to the north of the Great Wall had cold climate and were sparsely populated, and people relied on nomadic herding and hunting for a living. Through their labor and lifestyle these people became strong and hardy against the cold, forming a nomadic culture. The Khitans inhabited the pastures at the upper Liaohe River in the vast expanse of land in the north, where their lifestyle was based mainly on nomadic herding, farming, fishing and hunting. It was a lifestyle that led naturally to the unique *nabo* system of a traveling court that moved around as the seasons shifted.

契丹族捺钵制度的产生与尚武精神是分不开的。契丹人活动于苦寒多风的松漠地区，恶劣的自然环境使他们形成了强悍善斗的性格。这些记载都说明契丹族习于渔畋射猎与富于战斗的尚武精神，尤其是辽朝皇帝举行春捺钵和秋猎时的捕鹅、猎虎活动，参加者均为辽军中的精兵强将。《契丹风土歌》中描绘道："平沙软草天鹅肥，胡儿千骑晓打围。皂旗低昂围渐急，惊作羊角凌空飞。"契丹族捺钵制度的产生和发展，一方面是与其周边各族、中原汉族文化的交流、碰撞、融合有关，另一方面也是契丹族始终保持着其特有的本色，从而在中国北方广袤的大地上形成了独具特色的契丹四时捺钵制度，自然产生了契丹捺钵文化，且保留和传承了下来。

The emergence of the Khitan *nabo* system was inseparable from their martial spirit. The Khitans lived in the bitterly cold and windswept region of Songmo, where the severe natural environment helped form a national character that was tough and warlike. Written records indicate that the Khitans fished, hunted and fought with a warlike spirit. In fact, participants of the Liao emperor's spring *nabo* and autumn hunt for swans and tigers were all elite members of the Liao army. We find this stanza in the "Song of Khitan Customs": "Flat sand and soft grass find swans fat, and thousands of Khitan soldiers are busy hunting. Banners stay low and the siege tightens, as sheep horns blare across heaven and earth." The emergence and development of the Khitan *nabo* system were related to its cultural exchange, collision and fusion with surrounding ethnic groups and the Han Chinese in Central China on one hand. On the other hand, the Khitans had always maintained their distinct qualities, thus giving rise to the unique *nabo* system that was preserved and passed down through generations.

到了清代，渔猎文化依然得到了传承和延续。孝庄祖陵坐落于查干湖东岸长山镇明珠公园内，陵内有清代孝庄文皇后生父生母的墓碑。孝庄，即大玉儿，又名布木布泰，清初内蒙古科尔沁部贝勒寨桑之女，有"满蒙第一美女"之誉。《清史稿・外戚表》载："孝庄文皇后父寨桑，莽古斯子。顺治十一年五月壬辰，追赠和硕忠亲王。"

The fishing and hunting culture was passed down and continued in the Qing Dynasty. On the east bank of

Chagan Lake, in the Pearl Park of Changshan Township, stand the tombstone of the father and mother of Empress Xiaozhuangwen of the Qing Dynasty. Xiaozhuang, whose given name was Dayu'er and was also known as Bumbutai, was the daughter of Lord Zhaisang of the Horqin Mongol tribe. She was known as the "First Beauty of Manchuria and Mongolia" in the early Qing Dynasty. According to the "Pedigree of the Imperial Relatives on the Maternal Side" in the *Draft History of Qing*, "Empress Xiaozhuangwen's father was Zhaisang, son of Manggusi; he was posthumously conferred the title of Heshuo Prince Zhong on the day of *renchen* in May of the 11th year of Emperor Shunzhi's reign." The Empress's mother received the posthumous title of Lady Xian.

顺治十一年，赠太后父寨桑和硕忠亲王，母贤妃。忠亲王寨桑就是清世祖顺治皇帝外祖父，忠亲王贤妃，即顺治皇帝的外祖母。两人死后，于顺治十一年（1654年）五月，被皇帝追封为和硕忠亲王和贤妃。顺治十二年五月初七，按顺治皇帝及孝庄太后旨意，由寨桑夫妇的长孙和塔立碑于墓前。

Empress Xiaozhuangwen was the mother of Emperor Shunzhi. This meant that Prince Zhong was the maternal grandfather of Shunzhi, whereas Lady Xian was Shunzhi's maternal grandmother. After receiving the posthumous titles in the 11th year of Shunzhi's reign (1654), on May 7 of the following year, a tombstone was erected at their gravesite by their eldest grandson Heta by order of Emperor Shunzhi and his mother, Empress Dowager Xiaozhuang.

1.虔诚的祈祷，凝固的永恒（左1）

2.心灵的到达（右上2）

3.大法号歌颂着查干淖尔（右下3）

1.Pious Prayer Frozen in Eternity (Left)

2.A Spiritual Homecoming (Upper right)

3.Dharma Horn Eulogizing Chagan Nur (Lower right)

孝庄为何把父母的墓地选取在这里，意欲为何？相传在美丽辽阔的查干淖尔大草原上，布木布泰随她的父亲寨桑来到查干湖畔打猎、游玩，正巧皇太极奉努尔哈赤之命来到科尔沁。两支队伍不期而遇，布木布泰正与皇太极形成对视，皇太极看得入了神，那美丽的容貌一下把他吸引了，以至于有了一种莫名的兴奋和深切的思念。有情人终成眷属。天命十年（1626）初，年仅十三岁的布木布泰与四贝勒皇太极完婚，开始了她传奇般的人生经历……

Why did Xiaozhuang choose to bury her parents there? According to legend, on the beautiful vast grassland of Chagan Nur, Bumbutai went hunting one day with her father Zhaisang. It so happened that Abahai (who later became the second emperor of the Qing dynasty) had come to Horqin on the order of his father Nurhachi. By pure chance, the two parties met. When Bumbutai and Abahai exchanged glances, Abahai was immediately captivated by the beautiful Bumbutai, and he could not stop thinking about her afterwards. The two were married at the beginning of the 10th regnal year of Tianming (1626). Bumbutai, then 13, thus embarked on a legendary life...

大小颗粒，千年祝愿
Offerings are made to the gods that have blessed this activity for centuries.

摄影 / 闫来锁
Photograph by / Yan Laisuo

水草丰美的查干淖尔大草原成为孝庄文皇后永生难忘的回忆，她生养在科尔沁草原，她的美貌与才智均源于科尔沁草原。更令她难忘的是她在这里遇见了皇太极，因此改变了她的人生，使她经历后金及清初四代三朝的政治沧桑，辅佐三朝帝王，为清初政权的巩固，作出了杰出的贡献。因此，查干湖和查干淖尔大草原，无疑成为博尔济吉特氏家族的福地。于是父母死后，她便把墓地选择在美丽的查干湖畔。

风雪开始弥漫
In the Drifting Snow

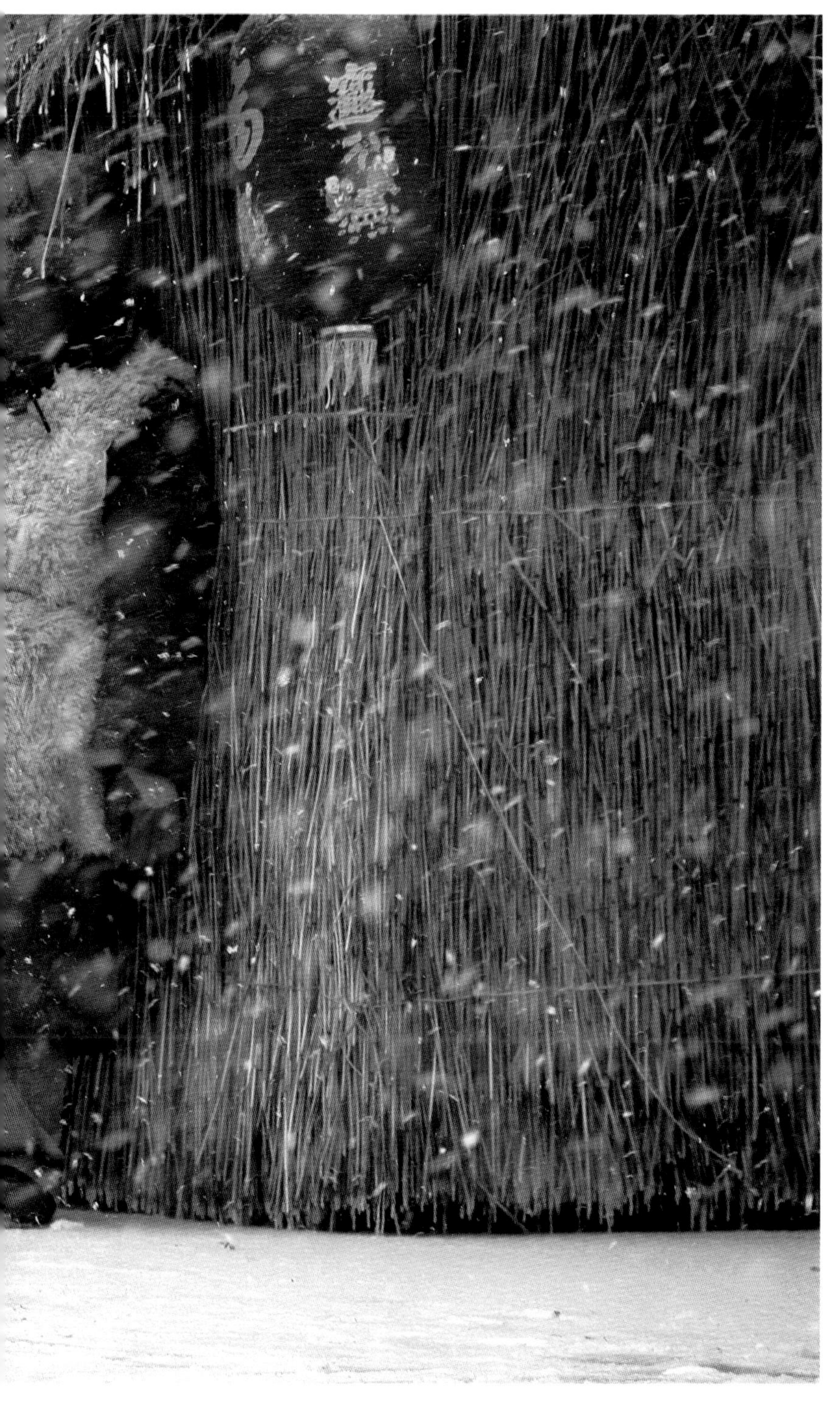

The lush Chagan Nur grassland became an unforgettable place for Empress Xiaozhuang. Not only was she born and raised on the Horqin Grassland, but, more indelibly, it was also here that she met Abahai, an event that changed her life forever. Because of that encounter, she would later experience the political vicissitudes that spanned four generations and three emperors in the late Jin and early Qing dynasties, assisting all three emperors and making outstanding contributions to the consolidation of the Qing regime. No doubt the Chagan Nur and the Chagan Nur grassland came to be seen as a blessed land for her family, the Boer Jijite clan. That was why she chose to bury her parents by the beautiful Chagan Lake.

在这里的冬季，人类充分地体会着生命对生命的亲近，也是生命对生命的承诺。在这里，人们有着深深的文化与心灵的遵循。冬季捕鱼需要网，在人们使用网前，先让沉睡了一春一夏的网从网库里“醒来”，这叫“醒”网。

醒网，是人以心的虔诚去唤醒人的亲密伙伴——网。此时，人们要集体来到放网的仓库里，面对那一堆堆沉睡了一春一夏的网，表示人类的虔诚，让它“醒”来。

醒来，是生命对“生命”的呼唤。

The people of Chagan Lake are guided by deeply rooted cultural and spiritual practices. Winter fishing requires nets, but before using the nets, people must "awaken" the nets kept in storage and have been dormant all through spring and summer.

Awakening the nets is to reverently rouse the fisherman's closest work partner. People gather at the storage, where piles of nets have slumbered from spring to summer, to awaken them with pious respect.

To awaken is for one life to call to another.

在祭湖与醒网仪式中人们会戴上面具，召唤过去

Masks are worn to invoke the past during the ceremony to worship the lake and "awaken" the nets.

走冰，那是心灵之路
Walking on the ice is also a spiritual journey.

人们要备好高香，在有网的仓库门口点燃，然后渔把头双手举握高香四面膜拜，口中念念有词："你沉睡一春一夏啦，现在该醒来了，振振精神，与我一起去吧，与我们一起作业！"

人们将手中的高香朝四方举拜，并喊着："东吉——东吉！西吉——西吉！开网大吉——！"

于是，人们这才把库房中的大网虔诚抬出，小心出门，装在早已等在门外的大车或爬犁上，拉向茫茫的查干淖尔冰面。

Fine incense is prepared and lit at the door of the net storage. With both hands, the fishing master raises the incense over his head and worships the four directions, chanting, "You have slumbered through spring and summer, now it is time to wake up and go to work with me!"

Holding the incense in their hands, people then worship the four directions, calling out: "Auspicious East – Auspicious East! Auspicious West – Auspicious West! Auspicious First Net!"

Only after that do the people carry out the big nets respectfully and carefully, load them onto the waiting carts or sledges outside the storage, and move towards the vast and frozen Chagan Nur.

查干淖尔久远的文化历程体现在它的祭湖醒网仪式上，并通过采集圣火、跳萨满舞和查玛舞、诵祭湖词和醒网词、捞头鱼等过程来实施。“醒”网祭湖仪式开始，由查干淖尔妙音寺的喇嘛虔诚地诵经，祷告湖神保佑渔夫们平安。

默默对话
A Silent Dialogue

北方的萨满师手舞皮鼓不停地敲打，并虔诚地诵念，然后围着敖包奔走。博（草原人称萨满为“博”）的到来连接了远古生命的呼唤，那是一种强大能力的回归，那是一种怯弱和软弱的消失，那是一种强悍性格的到来，那是一种美丽多元文化的释放，那是人对沉睡生命的唤醒，那是久远的岁月对人类虔诚的指点。博，活态地唤醒了岁月，使得大自然敞开胸怀接纳着生命的到来……这是一种古老的祭湖醒网仪式。

查玛舞是一种古老的原始图腾舞蹈，人们戴上各种动物和神灵的面具来演示说明一切逝去的都已复活。古朴苍凉的歌简洁而生动，舞蹈语言带有鲜明的自然特征，一切都充满经验性和历程感，这充分地向人表示查干淖尔的人们具备了很强的生存能力。

Chagan Nur’s long cultural history is mostly manifested in its ceremony of honoring the lake and awakening the nets. The ceremony is carried out through processes such as collecting the holy fire, dancing the shaman dance and the Chama dance, chanting the prayers in worship of the lake and to awaken the nets, and harvesting the first fish. The ceremony begins with pious chanting by lamas of the Miaoyin Temple in Chagan Nur, who pray for the lake god to bless the fishermen with safety.

The shaman strikes the leather drums while chanting piously, then runs around the *aobao* (a sacred stone heap used as an altar). The presence of the *bo* (the grassland people's term for shaman) forms a link to life in ancient times, invoking the return of powerful abilities, the disappearance of timidity and weakness, the emergence of a strong character, the release of a beautiful and diverse culture, the awakening of slumbering life, and the guidance offered by times long past. The *bo* brings the past back to life, and opens up nature to accept the arrival of life… Such is the ancient ceremony of worshipping the lake and awakening the nets.

The Chama dance is an ancient primitive totem dance, where people wear a variety of masks of animals and gods to demonstrate that all that have faded have been resurrected. The simple and desolate songs are succinct and vivid, and the dance contains distinct naturalistic features. Everything is experiential and gives the sense of time progressing, demonstrating the resilience of the people of Chagan Nur.

祭师来到供桌前端起一碗酒走到敖包旁，用蒙语诵祭湖词：

啊，长生天，先祖之灵；
庇护众生，求昌盛，求繁荣。
查干湖，天父的神镜；
查干湖，地母的眼睛——
啊，歌天唱地查玛舞，
鼓乐齐鸣诵经声。
举灯为心召日月，
满湖金银庆丰登。
一祭万世不老的天父！
再祭赐予我们生命的地母！
祭祀万灵的湖神，让湖神保佑查干湖连年有余、永世昌盛！

The priest comes to the sacrificial table, raises a bowl of liquor, walks to the *aobao*, and chants a Mongolian prayer in worship of the lake:

Ah, Eternal Heaven and Ancestral Spirits,
Shelter all beings, let us thrive and prosper.
Chagan Lake, the holy mirror of our Heavenly Father,
Chagan Lake, the eye of our Earth Mother
Ah, in honor of Heaven and Earth we sing and dance the Charma, we play music and chant prayers.
Hoist the lanterns as our hearts to call forth the sun and the moon,
Let the lake reflect gold and silver to celebrate a bumper harvest.
First we worship our eternal Heavenly Father!
Second we worship our life-giving Earth Mother!
Then we worship the almighty Lake God;
May the Lake God bless Chagan Lake with year after year of good harvest and prosperity forever!

这时渔把头手持哈达，带渔工走到祭坛前面的供桌前，端起供桌上的一碗酒，带领渔工走到祭坛旁装大网的爬犁前，面向大网单膝跪地双手抱拳，渔把头站在渔工队伍前，面向大网手捧酒碗，用蒙语诵醒网词：

At this point, holding the *hada* (ceremonial scarf), the fishing master leads the fishermen to the sacrificial table before the altar. He takes a bowl of liquor from the table and leads the fishermen to the sledge loaded with the large nets beside the altar. There, the fishermen kneel with one knee on the ground and hands folded, while the fishing master stands at the front of the procession, raises the bowl of liquor to the large nets, and chants the Mongolian prayer for awakening the nets :

啊，长生天，先祖之光；
日精月华，庆丰盈，祝辉煌。
查干湖，绿色的福地，
查干湖，黄金的储仓；
啊，圆圆至圣查干湖，
鱼山鱼海渔歌长。
捕鱼节上醒网喽，

祭山祭水祭太阳。

Ah, Eternal Heaven and Ancestral Light;
The brilliance of the sun and moon celebrates harvest and glory.
Chagan Lake, blessed green land,
Chagan Lake, golden treasure house.
Ah, round and most sacred Chagan Lake,
Teeming with mountains and seas of fish as the fishing song sings eternal.
At the Fishing Festival we awaken our nets,
As we worship the mountains, the waters and the sun!

伙计们，万灵的天父地母已经唤醒了沉睡的大网，万能的查干湖神赐予我们力量，我们该饱肚准备进湖了。

感谢长生天赐予的力量，感谢万灵的湖神！

伙计们，喷香的奶干添力量，醇香的奶酒增豪情，咱们今年冬捕，一定收红网！伙计们，干！

众渔工齐呼：收红网去了！

冬捕的欢庆的鞭炮点燃了，火光在空中炸开。渔把头跳上拖网的大车，当驱马的响鞭在寒冷的旷野上空炸开的时候，祭网的壮行酒下肚的温热还在心底滚烫，北方马儿已踏着湖面的冰雪奔跑，查干淖尔壮丽的冬捕开始了。

Mates, the almighty Heavenly Father and Earth Mother have awakened the big sleeping nets, and the almighty Chagan Lake God has given us strength. Let us eat and prepare ourselves to march to the lake.

争先恐后的等待

Anticipating the long-awaited harvest.

Thank you, Eternal Heaven, for giving us strength!

Thank you, almighty Lake God!

Mates, the tasty milk cubes have boosted our strength, and the mellow fermented milk has lifted our spits. Our winter fishing this year is bound to see a bumper harvest. Mates, let's go!

All the fishermen shout in unison: Let's go for the bumper harvest!

The firecrackers celebrating the winter fishing are set off, exploding in the air with sparks of fire. The fishing master jumps onto the cart pulling the nets. As the crack of the whip sounds in the cold air of the wilderness, the horses begin to run. With the liquor from the net awakening ceremony still burning hot inside the fishermen, the northern horses are already galloping across the ice and snow of the lake surface. The magnificent winter fishing of Chagan Nur has begun.

ICE HERITAGE

冰原遗产

冰镩镩冰的一瞬间，

银色的冰块和白色的冰沫随着冰镩起落飞舞跳跃，

太阳的光芒透过晶莹的冰块折射出闪闪的光柱和亮点，

无论人从哪个角度看去都像到了一个神话传说中的万宝坡，

遍地的奇珍异宝在闪闪发亮，

冰凌带着太阳的五色光泽在闪烁着。

When the ice chisel breaks ice,
the silvery ice and white ice foam dance with the chisel's
upward and downward movements.
Sunlight penetrates and is refracted by the crystal ice into
columns of light and bright spots.
From whatever angle you see this,
it will seem like you have entered the land of treasures in myths and legends.
Where rare treasures glisten everywhere,
and ice spikes glitter in the sunlight's many colors.

每步行走，一生追求

Taking one step at a time in a lifelong pursuit.

冬季，寒冷在宁静中被放大，传递着一种久远的神奇，冰雪的波浪在荒寒的土地上凝固成平静，扩展为一种神圣。空旷的地平线弥漫着一种浓郁的神秘，仿佛在向人娓娓动听地讲述一个生命的故事。可是生命在哪，荒冷的冰野仿佛不见一丝生命的痕迹。当人细心去倾听地表以上秋水冻成的冰坝和寒冷凝固的雪线下晶莹的冰野，那里却正传递出一种远古的呼唤。

In winter, the cold is amplified in the quiet, conveying a sense of long-ago wonders; the ice and snow solidify on the cold barren land, forming an expanse that is calm and silent, even sacred. The vast and empty horizon is filled with a deep sense of mystery, as though it has a story about life to tell. But where is the life? The desolate ice field seems to betray no trace of life. And yet, when people listen carefully to the ice dams formed by the frozen autumn waters and the ice field formed by the accumulation of frozen snow, an ancient call seems to beckon.

冰冻的旷野给予生命走进生命的角度，这块仿佛静止的冰野其实是人了解生命的机会。查干淖尔的生命之门一旦开启，有心人便会一下子扑进大自然原野的怀抱。千百年来，寒冬在这片土地上留下了独特而灿烂的记忆，这是它自己的记忆，区别于一切记忆。也许是地球和大自然的一份偶然厚爱，使查干淖尔避开了现代社会的侵扰，它尽情地享受着属于自己的寒冷和宁静。

The frozen wilderness, with its seeming stillness, in fact provides an angle from which human life can understand other life forms. Once the door to life in Chagan Nur opens, those willing to can abandon themselves to the embrace of the natural wilderness. For thousands of years, the frigid winter has left its unique and brilliant imprint on this land. Perhaps purely by chance, Chagan Nur has been favored and protected by nature, remaining free from the interference of modern society, enjoying the cold and quiet that is all its own.

洞穿脚下的坚冰，人要在漫无边际的冰原上不停地迁徙，让冰扎(一种带线绳的工具)去丈量无边的冰野。贴在怀里的巨大的闪着寒光的冰镩是查干淖尔

渔夫的神笔，用不了多久，他们便用它在这片冰原上书写他们的生存史。

当把头丈量好冰眼距离和位置，三大道工序凿冰眼便开始了。每两个人凿一个冰眼。先凿一个大冰眼叫“下网眼”……

To see through the ice below their feet, people must keep moving on the endless ice field, using the ice gauge (a tool attached to a rope) to measure the boundless expanse. The big, glistening ice chisels that the fishermen at Chagan Nur carry are like magic pens with which they will soon write the story of their survival on the icy land.

When the fishing master has measured the distance and locations of the ice "eyes" (holes in the ice), the fishermen begin the three-part process of chiseling ice eyes. Two people work together to chisel an ice eye. First they chisel a large ice eye called the "net-casting eye"...

冬捕时冰上的工具又多又复杂，其中最重要的一件叫冰镩。在人类进化史上复杂工具的发明表明了人类走出了晚期智人的时期而进入了智慧期。这种冰镩是由当地的铁匠专门打制的破冰工具，由镩头、镩墩子和镩拐子三部分组成。一把冰镩有二三十公斤重，这样才能“镩冰”“炸冰”。冰镩的尖十分坚利，闪着如冰一样的寒光。

The tools for the winter fishing are many and complex, the most important of which is the ice chisel. In the history of human evolution, the invention of complex tools marked the point at which modern, intelligent humans emerged from late *Homo sapiens*. The ice chisel is made by local blacksmiths for the specific purpose of breaking ice. It is composed of three parts: Chisel head, chisel block and chisel frame. An ice chisel weighs as much as 20 to 30 kilograms, allowing it to chip ice and "blow up ice". The tip of the ice chisel is very sharp, and glistens like the cold ice.

冰镩镩冰的一瞬间，银色的冰块和白色的冰沫随着冰镩起落飞舞跳跃，太阳的光芒透过晶莹的冰块折射出闪闪的光柱和亮点，无论人从哪个角度看去都像到了一个神话传说中的万宝坡，遍地的奇珍异宝在闪闪发亮，冰凌带着太阳的五色光泽在闪烁着。

When the ice chisel breaks ice, the silvery ice and white ice foam dance with the chisel's upward and downward movements. Sunlight penetrates and is refracted by the crystal ice into columns of light and bright spots. From whatever angle you see this, it will seem like you have entered the land of treasure in myths and legends, where rare treasures glisten everywhere, and ice spikes glitter in the sunlight's many colors.

在查干淖尔，渔民使的网叫麻网。麻网是用麻的纤维编制而成。麻，本来是北方平原上一种常见的植物，它喜欢生长在田间地头，又分花麻和线麻。花麻又叫宽叶荨麻，蒙语为“哈拉海”，夏秋季往往散发出一阵阵浓郁的药香味儿。查干淖尔草甸上生长着成片这种荨麻，渔民常常把这种植物采来，熬水喝以治惊风，可解毒并通风。特别是捕鱼寒苦，这种植物可祛风湿。而线麻又叫大麻，长得很高，出土不久便散发着一股浓浓的清香花味儿。秋季的时候，渔民们把麻割下来，成捆地使车拉回去，投放到村中大水坑里去沤，俗称“沤麻”。麻经过沤发，外皮就会从秆上脱离，这就是皮麻。皮麻经过干燥晾晒、捶压、梳理等阶段，使其中柔软的纤维突露出来成为“麻”。于是人们把麻打成麻捆或麻卷儿，这仅是制网的前期。

In Chagan Nur, fishermen use the hemp net, so called because it is woven from hemp fibers. Hemp is a common plant on China's northern plains, found mostly in farmland. There are two kinds of hemp, the flower hemp and the thread hemp. The flower hemp, also known as the wide-leaf nettle, and "harahai" in Mongolian, often exudes strong bursts of medicinal fragrance in summer and fall. This kind of nettle grows in large swathes in the marshlands of Chagan Nur. Fishermen often gather this plant, boil it in water and drink it to treat convulsions. It also has the effects of detoxification, boosting body circulation, and, perhaps more importantly for fishermen who work in bitter cold conditions, helping to alleviate rheumatism. The thread hemp plant, also known as big hemp, grows very tall, and exudes a thick floral fragrance soon after sprouting. In autumn, fishermen cut it, bundle it and haul it back in carts. It is then placed in the village's retting pond for what is commonly known as "hemp retting". The hemp bark that separates from the stalk after retting is called skin hemp. The skin hemp goes through processes that include drying, beating, combing, etc., to reveal its soft fiber, which is then bundled into coils. And this is only the preparation for making fish nets.

为了织网，还要把麻披纺成茎，就是一种细线，缠在“线桄子”上，以便织“网片”。捕鱼要用很多的“绳”，但绳不叫绳，细的叫“水线”，粗的叫“绦”。大绦，就是大绳。冬捕时一趟网有两根大绦，每根长三十三丈，还有诸多小绳。大绦是根吃力的绳索。冬捕网下到冰底，拖上来的网裹着鱼有上万斤的分量，加上吃水后绳的分量就更重，所以大绦的质量非常的讲究。从前这根大绦往往由捕鱼部落里的打绳能手“绳匠”来打制，如果网队太多，绳匠被各网队抢来抢去，就只好到镇上请专门的绳匠来打大绦。

To make the fishing nets, the skin hemp must be spun into strands, which are then wrapped around the "line reel" to be woven into the "mesh". Fishing requires a lot of rope, but the rope is not referred to as rope; the thin ones are called water lines and the thick ones are called "braids". A large braid refers to a large rope. The nets used in winter fishing consist of two large braids, each of which is around 110 meters in length, in addition to many small ropes. The large braids must be able to withstand heavy force. During winter fishing, when the nets are hauled up from under the ice, they often contain some 5000 kilograms of fish, and the ropes have become heavier with water, so great importance is placed on the

摄影 / 刘玉忱
Photograph by / Liu Yuchen

哥仨日夜轮岗，守望古老冰原
Three brothers take shifts to keep watch over the ancient ice field.

quality of the large braids. In the past, large braids were often made by rope masters of the fishing tribes. When there were too many fishing teams and not enough rope masters to go around, people had to go into town to ask professional rope makers for help with the large braids.

春季的查干淖尔，天还是出奇的冷，可查干淖尔渔夫们却集体在寒冷空旷的荒原上一齐扭着腰身，一齐叫喊着给绳车子上劲打麻绳。声音是：啊呦！啊呦！很好听，却又非常的单调。可是这却使沉睡了一冬的查干淖尔热闹起来了。

Even in springtime it is still surprisingly cold in Chagan Nur, and yet the fishermen have gathered in the frigid wilderness, collectively twisting their torsos and calling out asthey make twisted hemp rope using the rope machine. They are calling out:“Ah Yo! Ah Yo!” It is a nice sound, though monotonous, but with this sound Chagan Nur seems to suddenly come alive after a long winter’s slumber.

在查干淖尔，渔夫们的女人是极其辛苦的，别看冬捕时的习俗是不许女人上冰，可是后勤的种种活计十分繁重，不用说给男人们做饭、看家这些事了，单是打麻绳也是她们繁重的体力劳动，几乎一年四季，渔夫的女人们都在做着这个活计。渔夫人家家家的房上都挂着一个叫“纺锤”的东西，纺锤悬着一绺麻披，女人就是烧火做饭和哄孩子睡觉的空档，也要忙于转动纺锤打麻绳，然后把一捆捆的细麻绳积攒起来，留着给男人做鞋和织鱼网。再就是通过纺车来“纺麻”，纺成绳用来编织鱼网和打大絛。这种网，都是经过查干淖尔渔夫认真“血”过，才行。一趟大网，往往要用一缸的猪血，少了浸不过来，这样网不好使，不防水。

In Chagan Nur, the fishermen's wives have a busy life. Though women are not allowed on the ice during the winter fishing, as the custom dictates, the logistics involve heavy and demanding work. Cooking and housekeeping are a given, on top of which the women are responsible for making hemp ropes, a heavy manual labor that keeps them busy almost year-round. A spindle hangs in every fisherman's house, and a tuft of hemp skin hangs from the spindle. In their spare time between cooking and taking care of their children, women are busy turning spindles to make hemp ropes, which they coil up and save to make shoes and weave fish nets for their men. Another job of the women is to "spin hemp" on the spinning wheel to make ropes for fishing nets and large braids. Once made, these nets must be carefully "blooded" by the Chagan Nur fishermen before they can be put to use. It usually takes a whole vat of pig blood to soak the large net thoroughly; otherwise the nets will not be waterproof and won't be handy to use.

雪网的过程，就像一场古老的戏剧，在北方的平原上，在查干淖尔渔夫中一代一代流传。特别是在凉秋季节，北方草原阳光充足，风也清凉。刚刚蘸完猪血的网，铺撒在平原草尖上晒，网一片片地在阳光下闪着亮光，很有韵味。

巧妙配器，演奏岁月之歌
Wonderful instruments in an age-old pursuit.

The net blooding process is like an ancient drama, passed down from generation to generation among the Chagan Nur fishermen on the northern plains. In the cool autumn, when the northern grassland is sunny and the breezes are cool but pleasant, the sight of the newly "blooded" nets laid out to dry on the grass, with the nets glistening under the sunlight, can be quite enchanting.

网在冰下布开，全靠穿杆的“劲”。这个“劲”，是向前穿动的“力”。这个“劲”和“力”，就是站在冰面上的渔夫用“扭矛”和“走钩”给它“上劲”——给力。

其实“给力”这个词，不是今天社会“发明”的，也不是小青年在生活的时尚中创造出来的，它在远古的查干淖尔冬捕的岁月中早已产生，它是人类早已存在的渔猎文化遗产的代表词。

When the fish nets are deployed under the ice, this is done by the force—a forward thrust—applied to the net pole. The force is applied by the fishermen on the ice through the tech-niques of "twisting spear" and "walking hook", a process kn-own as *geili* (giving force) in Chinese.

Thus, the term *ge-ili* (used in contem-

升腾起来的是太阳光芒的结晶
Chipped ice dances in the sunlight.

porary Chinese society to mean "cool" or "awesome") is not a modern "invention", nor was it coined by the fashionable young people. It had come into being in the long-ago days of winter fishing at Chagan Nur, and represents a fishing cultural heritage that has existed since ancient times.

当网从下网眼"堆"下去时，渔夫们就开始给穿杆"给力"了。这种给穿杆加力，是一种绝活，全靠技术。首先，当把巨大的带着水线的杆子顺入冰下后，"扭矛"要搭住穿杆的一头，然后以手腕的"巧劲"一扭，一下子使穿杆起动了。

When the net is "piled down" from the net casting "eye", the fishermen begin to apply force to the net pole. This is a unique technique that relies entirely on skill. First, when the huge pole with water lines attached to it slides into the water under the ice, those responsible for "twisting spear" must hold one end of the pole and use the "dexterous force" of the wrist to give it a twist, setting the pole in motion.

水下的物体，其实浮力是非常重要的。当扭矛"一打"，那种"劲"迅速过渡到杆上，杆便运行起来。这种"打劲法"，年轻的渔夫望尘莫及。而经验娴熟的老渔把头已干了一辈子"走杆"了。他的"劲"，全在"心"上。看起来他用手，用胳膊，其实是在用"心灵"去打杆。打杆使劲，要猛一打，不能打"滑了"。

For objects that are under water, buoyancy is crucial. With the "twisting of the spear", the force applied is quickly transferred to the pole, which begins to move. This technique, which the veteran fishing master has practiced all his life, is not something that the young fishermen can easily master. The way he applies force comes from his heart. It may seem like he is using his hands and arms, but, in fact, he is working the pole with his mind. Working the pole requires a decisive move, and you cannot afford to "slip".

所谓的打滑了，是指你在转动"扭矛"时没有掌握好"发力"的技巧，这时"一打"，劲消耗在"传递"上，杆没有受到力。而"打杆"的一瞬间，要在"扭"上下功夫。杆要前行，劲要"横"打，如何产生"前行力"，全靠人去用心琢磨"起动杆"和"加速杆"的时间和力度。起动杆时的"打劲"和"加速杆"时的"打劲"完全是两回事，而且，扭矛掐在杆的什么位置上，都很讲究。

Slip means failing to apply force with the right technique while twisting the pole, resulting in the force not traveling to the pole. The trick lies in the twisting. To make the pole move forward, the force must be applied horizontally. How to produce the force that causes the pole to move forward is entirely dependent on the careful timing and control of force applied when "launching the pole" and "accelerating the pole"; the force applied to achieve the two types of motion is completely different. There is also a specific spot where one needs to hold the pole during the twisting.

能力和技艺是这种渔猎遗产的重要标志。人类需要传承的，正是这种珍贵的技艺文化遗产。这是查干淖尔遗产。别土无有，别土不生。

一个姿态，雪原遗产

A stance that speaks of a legacy on the fields of ice.

Abilities and skills are important symbols of this fishing heritage. It is exactly this kind of invaluable cultural heritage that humans must inherit and pass down. And the heritage of Chagan Nur is a unique one found nowhere else on earth.

在人们一般意义的理解上，捕鱼只要把网向空中抛开，网缓缓地落下，罩住水面，再一提一拉，一网鱼就拖上来了。这其实只是人们对夏季渔猎生活的一般性理解。而查干淖尔冬捕，在严寒的冬季那种冰下的网，不能像夏天那样高高抛起，轻轻落下，它要在冰层下慢慢地“布”开。谁来“布”？表面上看是网自己在分布。而其实这种分布，是靠人以智慧（文化遗产）来“指挥”网去自动展开并捕捞鱼，这是一件多么神奇的事情呢！

People generallyu nderstand fishing as such: Cast the net into the air; the net falls slowly onto the water surface; then all you need to do is lift and pull, and you will have yourself a net full of fish. In fact, this is just a generic understanding associated with summer fishing. During winter fishing in Chagan Nur, one cannot expect the net, cast high into the air, to fall gently into the water as in summer; instead, it must be “spread” slowly under the ice. Who does the spreading? On the surface, it may seem as though the net is spreading by itself. In fact, it is the result of human ingenuity (cultural heritage), which “commands” the net to spread on its own and to capture fish. How truly marvelous!

这种网，成为“组合”网。平时不是一个整体，因为冰下的空间太大。冬捕的网，要分成若干“块”。冬捕渔网一趟网由96块网组成，总长度为600丈，网高三丈三。网，像鸟的翅膀，所以又叫“网翅”。那将是怎样的巨网潜伏在茫茫雪原的冰层之下。冰雪之下，真的是“布”开了“天罗地网”……

The net used for winter fishing is a "combination" net. It is normally not put together in its entirety because it is so big. All told, a winter fishing net consists of 96 individual nets, with a total length of close to 2000 meters and a height of about 10 meters. The net is like a bird's wing, so it is also known as "net wing". Imagine this giant net lurking under the ice on the snowy field and how inescapable it must be...

网垛在冰原上，恰似一座座石头山峰。而山峰上，站立着一个个渔夫。那是一种奇特的人网的组合。世上有各种网，但绝没有如查干淖尔这样的网，"一网"就堆成一座山。

网山在茫茫的冰原上起浮，像远处的山岗。一座座山岗紧相连啊，查干淖尔，连绵起伏的网山把久远的传奇从远古传述至今天。

The piles of net stand like mountain peaks of actual rocks on the ice, and on top of each peak stands a fisherman. It is a strange combination of men and nets. There are many kinds of nets in the world, but nowhere are the nets like those at Chagan Nur, where a net makes a mountain.

The net piles undulate on the vast ice, just like the distant hills. Oh, Chagan Nur, where the rolling net hills stand and speak of ancient legends still alive today.

浓烈的金光照亮了浩渺的查干淖尔，地表上的网山一点点被冰层张开的大口所吞噬。在人的脚下，在那五光十色的太阳光照射下的晶莹的冰下，人们可以清晰地看到大湖的细胞和血管——网，那鲜明的网丝在漂动，在远去。

The strong golden light illuminates the vast Chagan Nur. The net heaps on the ice surface are swallowed little by little by the gaping holes. Beneath the feet that stand on the ice, beneath the ice illuminated by the sunlight, the great lake's cells and blood vessels can be clearly seen as the net, with the distinctive fibers floating in the water, slowly drifts far, far away.

摄影 / 闫来锁
Photograph by / Yan Laisuo

时刻准备——迁徙
Always ready and on the move

凛冬时节，古老的查干淖尔冰面闪着灰色的光泽，那是天空的乌云把雪原涂成了这种颜色。如果太阳不出来，一冬天都是这样，可是渔夫们能透过天和冰面的颜色去断定拉网时刻。

In the height of winter, when the age-old ice of Chagan Nur glistens with gray luster, it is the dark clouds in the sky that have painted the snow field this color. If the sun does not come out, it will be like this the whole winter. However, by looking at the colors of the sky and the ice surface, the fishermen are able to judge when to bring in the nets.

冬天，冰面上奇寒无比。网和绳上的水把他们身上淋湿，又冻成冰壳。查干淖尔渔夫一个个就成了会移动的“冰雕”。

当穿杆瞬间插入厚厚的冰层时，人们也在寻思，这一网下去，谁知多少万斤呢？

千百年了，查干淖尔曾有多少次这样把“杆子”插进冰层去，也插进了人们自己深深的记忆之中？而大绦又从岁月的底层把记忆拉出来，连接成一段难忘的记忆。

It is extremely cold on the ice in winter. The water on the net and the ropes splashes onto the men, then freezes, forming an ice crust over them. In this way, the Chagan Nur fishermen become walking ice sculptures.

As the pole is inserted into the thick layer of ice, the people are also wondering: How many kilograms will they fetch from this catch?

Over thousands of years, Chagan Nur has seen the pole inserted into the ice countless times, a scene that has also become deeply rooted in people's memories. Soon, the big braid rope will also bring up memories from times past, another link in a chain of unforgettable memories.

一冬天，要穿坏几件老羊皮袄。多少次的生死使他们领略了查干淖尔的威力，终于让一个人的生命放射出奇异的光芒，成为冰原人。

冰原人，有自己的生命认识，马儿就和他自己一样。当寒风把人冻得合不上嘴巴，他依然要掰着冻得张不开马儿的嘴，把温热的料填入“伙计”的肚里。

查干淖尔，是生命与生命真诚碰撞的土地。

How many sheepskin coats will they wear out over one winter? Time and time again, living on the edge of life and death has made them appreciate the power of Chagan Nur. And finally, a person's life glows with an extraordinary light, and he has become a man of the ice field.

The people of the ice field have their own take on life. To them, the horses are to be treated just like themselves. When the cold wind so freezes them that they cannot close their mouths,and the horses are so cold that they can barely open their mouths, still the men will pry open the horses' mouths to send warm feed into the stomachs of their "partner".

大网如果在冰下布开，可想而知，茫茫的几百平方公里的冰下，那网已经展开，由穿杆带动，一点点地运行到了“出网口”了。出网口，其实和下网口的功能一样，是网由此出来的口。但不同的是，这个网不是空网，而是“实”网了。实，就是“红”，又叫“日头冒红网”。这是指网从夜里和黎明开始下网，到当天的早上，也有中午或下晌，就开始起网了。

With the large net spread under the ice, one can imagine the net extending under the vast ice of hundreds of square kilometers and, pulled by the pole, moves little by little towards the hole for extracting the net. Like the net casting hole, it is an opening on the ice, only the net that passes through it won’t be empty, but will be “solid”. A solid net is a “red” net, also known as the “red sunrise net”. This is because after the net is cast at night or dawn, it is hauled up the following morning, sometimes at noon or in the afternoon on the same day.

其实，那网一直也没有停，它是在不停地运行，现在，已来到了出网眼了。但是，它太沉重了。因为有“鱼”，人们丰收的果实在里边，一般的力气是拉不动的。怎么办呢？这时，人类要感谢动物了。

人，无时无刻不在歌唱，让赞歌在心底升腾……
人，无时无刻不在舞动，让脚步踏醒沉睡的荒原……
这里永远是生命体验生命的地方。
这里有无数的迷人的、超自然的想象。

In fact, that net has never stopped; it is always in motion. Now it has come to the extraction hole. However, it is heavywith fish, the fruits of the fishermen's labors. It cannot be pulled up by mere human strength. What to do? This is when the animals come in.

People are singing all the time. Let their hymns rise from the bottom of their heart...
People are dancing all the time. Let their footsteps wake up the sleeping wilderness...
It is forever a place where life experiences life.
There are countless fascinating and supernatural imaginings here.

沉入冰下的网，打开了人类梦想的大门，生命走进这扇大门，让无数的记忆复活。记忆之网，打捞出沉淀的往昔岁月，无限的生命精华，数不尽的思想珍宝，灿烂的多彩的文化内涵，一切的一切都收入到这巨大的网中……

The net sinking into the ice opened the door to human dreams, and life entered through this door, resurrecting countless memories. The net of memories digs up the sediments of years past, the infinite wonders of life, the countless treasures of thought, and bright and colorful cultural meanings. Everything is collected by this vast net...

网，还在徐徐地运行，它连接了天地的存在，使得自然和生命天衣无缝。其实它是在梳理，它梳理着自然的走向，梳理着生命的脉搏，梳理着精神的光芒，梳理着生命的风采，还有永远梳理不尽的记忆……

The net is still moving, slowly. It connects the existence of heaven and earth, seamlessly bringing together nature and life. In fact, it combs through the trends of nature, the pulses of life, the spark of spirits, the wonders of life, and the endless memories...

冬捕是人类从冰下去捕捞鱼的一种自然活动，人们知道“鱼”在冰层之下，这种举动的目的十分明确。可是，这种对鱼的打捞其实是直奔人们认识到的一个主题，人们在完成对鱼的打捞的同时，往往更加注意对另一种珍贵的“载体”的打捞，那就是渔猎文化的打捞。

Winter fishing is a natural human activity with a clear purpose: To catch the fish that people know are under the ice. However, this activity points directly to another theme, and that is the exploration and understanding of the precious fishing culture from which the activity originates.

千百年来，人在自然之中生存，其实就是一个认识自然、了解自然、依赖自然而活的过程，查干淖尔渔夫处处注意这样去生存……

Humans have lived in nature for millennia. It is in fact a process of getting to know nature, understanding nature and relying on nature to survive. The Chagan Nur fishermen are experts at living this way...

查干淖尔，那是一片气息清凉的土地。这是渔夫们世代保持下来的一种璀璨生存习惯。渔具在查干淖尔一年四季都有不同的种类，在这里，查干淖尔应该是人类的查干淖尔。它的许多发明和创造深深地被那些奇特的渔具记载下来，传承下来了。每年秋冬，北风把四野一吹，查干淖尔就进入自己独特的冬捕之日了，这时，这里诸多的冬捕渔猎工具就要派上自己的用场了。这些工具不是现用现做，许多时候，工具在一春一夏早已准备好了。

Chagan Nur is a land of cool and refreshing air, and here the fishermen have maintained a brilliant way of life through generations. Fishing gears in Chagan Nur vary from season to season, and these unique tools have also served to record and preserve the ingenuity of the people here. In autumn and winter each year, when the north wind starts to blow, Chagan Nur enters the season of winter fishing, when the many fishing tools will be put to their proper use. That is not to say that the tools will be made only then; in fact, in many cases they have been ready long since spring and summer.

查干淖尔的文化表述在它的存在和生动的传承上，马轮子就是其一。今天我们看到的马轮子有些已是钢筋铁管焊制的了。但在从前，打鱼人完全使用粗硬的树木去制作，样子和现在马轮子形状一样。这是使用查干淖尔草甸沙原上的一种蒙古黄榆木来制作的马轮子，结实而且耐用，抗造，这些优良品质来自于黄榆的生命之本。

Much of the culture of Chagan Nur is expressed in its very existence and vivid material inheritance, the horse winch being one such example. Today's horse winches are made of welded steel bars and pipes. However, in the old days, fishermen made horse winches entirely out of hard wood, and it was shaped just like those that exist today. The wood used was a kind of Mongolian elm from the marshland and sandy plains of Chagan Nur, making the winch strong and durable, thanks to the excellent qualities of the elm.

我们发现了一个重要的规律：冰镩，高三尺三；扭矛，高三尺九；走勾，高六尺六；冰崩子，高六尺六；抄捞子，高六尺六；穿杆，长三丈三；大绦，长三十三丈；水线，长一百三十三丈,这些工具的尺寸都奇异地统一在“三”“六”“九”上。于是，我们惊醒了，原来古老的查干淖尔一直在传承着中华民族灿烂的传统文化，保留着这种原生态文化，因为“三”是天、地、人的基数；“六”为六六大顺；“九”乃九九归一。查干淖尔渔猎保留了中华民族灿烂的文化基因。

We have discovered an important rule: The ice chisel stands at 3.3 *chi* (1.1 meters); the twisting spear is 3.9 *chi* (1.3 meters) tall; the traveling hook is 6.6 *chi* (2.2 meters) tall, as are the ice bow and the ladle; the net pole is 3.3 *zhang* (11 meters) in length; the big braid is 33 *zhang* (110 meters) long; the water line measures at 133 *zhang* (443 meters)—somehow, the measurements of these tools all have the numbers 3, 6 and 9. Suddenly we realized that the traditions of Chinese culture have been inherited by Chagan Nur, which has preserved its original cultural ecology. The number 3 is the base number of the sky, the earth and men; 6 stands for a Chinese saying that means everything will go smoothly; 9 indicates a return to the original state. As such, the Chagan Nur fishing community has retained the finest DNA of Chinese culture.

抄捞子，专门用来抄冰洞里的冰和鱼。搭勾是“搭网”所用，这些抄捞子是冰上的常规工具，在冬季的冰上，它们的网和把上，都结着厚冰和寒霜。

The ladle is specifically used to catch ice fragments and fish in thc icc hole. The hook is used for netting. The ladle is a common tool on ice. On the ice in winter, its net and handle are always covered with thick ice and frost.

在严寒的北方，它们和渔人一样，是在严寒中生存的生死伙伴。它们不会说话。如果会，它们也会像人类一样去叙述查干淖尔生动的历程和文化……

在北方人的生活中，许多时候人们都在遵循着一种习惯，劳累时不能坐在工具上休息，说这是对工具的不尊。北方的人认为，一旦人不尊重工具，工具就再也不为你出力了。

仅仅是喘息
A short break

In the cold north, these tools, like the fishermen, are partners surviving in the cold. They do not speak. If they did, they would tell the vivid history and culture of Chagan Nur...

The northerners follow a habit: Even when tired, they do not sit on a tool for rest, because that would mean disrespect for the tool. The northerners believe that once you fail to respect the tools, the tools will no longer work for you.

表面看，这好像是人自己的思想。但只要细细想来，人认定了一种思想，一点点地传承下来，这就是民俗了。民俗中包含着的道理恰恰是一种非常有用的道理。因为不去“坐”自己使用的工具本身喻含着一种尊重自己的道理。所以工具，应该是人自己的情感。查干淖尔人就是这样的人。

On the surface, this seems to be something that people thought up. However, further reflection will show that when people form and hold on to an idea, which is passed down through time, it gradually becomes a folk custom. The idea contained in this folk custom happens to be a very useful one, for refraining from sitting on their own tools contains connotations of self-respect. The tools, therefore, represent people's own sentiments. The people of Chagan Nur are just such people.

这些工具，都是一种渔猎文化记忆的重要载体。鱼叉子是在冰上撮鱼用的。那种长长的齿是为了不伤着鱼肉，保持鱼的完整。冬天在冰上，鱼肉发脆，一碰就碎。冰杖子是用来推冰和丈量打冰眼的距离的用具。平板鱼撮子是把冰冻的鱼攒堆时所用。

These tools are important vessels of memories of the fishing culture. On the ice in winter, fish flesh is brittle and easily broken. The fishing fork used to gather fish on ice has long teeth that are designed to avoid damaging the fish flesh, keeping the fish intact. The ice stick is used to push ice and measure distances while making ice holes. The flat-plate shovel is used to lift and pile frozen fish.

在查干淖尔，铁匠是重要的能手。长短锤，钳子，各类长短把剪子，还有铁铗子等等都是他的伙伴。我们常常感觉到，查干淖尔往往就是生活的直接记载和保留。一切都带有浓浓的生活与自然的气息，是一种生存的原色气息。

In Chagan Nur, the blacksmith is an important workman. His partners are long and short hammers, pliers, scissors of varied lengths, iron clips, etc. Chagan Nur often gives the sense that it is recording and preserving a way of life. Everything carries a thick atmosphere of life and nature. It is a kind of life in its original state.

深冬，查干淖尔的冰原在欢腾着，这是因为冰原上有马轮子在欢转。如果说查干淖尔与世上许多生存行为有所不同，冰上马轮子便是最为生动的一幕。你看看吧，马儿浑身披着厚厚的寒霜，它们在冰上转圈奔跑着，已经成了“霜马”，赶马轮子的人用手中的长鞭，时而抽出清脆的鞭响。那种鞭响在空旷的雪野上炸开，传向无垠的寒雪茫茫的雪原。这种景致只有这里存在，也是查干淖尔的独创。

It is deep in the winter, but there is jubilation on the ice field of Chagan Nur as the horse winches turn. It is the most vivid scene in a way of life that is different from many other ways of life in other parts of the world. See for yourself: The horses, covered with thick frost, gallop in circles on the ice as the drivers crack their whips from time to time. The sharp sound explodes over the snow and travels throughout the vast land of whiteness. This is a scene that can only be seen here, a unique Chagan Nur experience.

冬捕前，其实许多冬捕细节已经开始。首先渔场要把院子浇水冻冰变成冰院子。冰院子是来自于水院子，这是北方一种大车店的名字。早些年，在靠近松花江、鸭绿江、嫩江、图们江沿岸的地方，一到冬季，严寒就使这些江河封冻了，山道岗道落雪不好走，于是这些冰封的江面就成了车马爬犁的康庄大道。特别是一到年跟前，山里和平原深处的人家都纷纷套上大车，装满各种特产黄烟、蘑菇、兽皮、松子、榛子、野鸡、山兔、大豆、杂粮、冻鱼、冻豆腐、粉条子，一车车、一爬犁一爬犁地顺着这些冰冻的大江奔往城镇的集市而来，从集市上换回烧纸、香码、糖块、面碱、布料、成衣、碗筷、蜡烛、年画等一应“年货”，再从这种大道返回村落过年祭祖接神。由于严寒使北方的江河封冻，江面上变成坦途可以走车马爬犁，这一下子催生了一门生意——冰上大车店水院子。水院子，其实是冰院子，是指建在江河边上专门接待从四面八方由此经过的运载山里山外货物的那些赶车的老客。冰院子大车店和普通的车店一样，备有热乎乎的大炕，各种饭食，吃完饭了还可以听二人转和北方的民间小戏。院子里专门有人夜里给马添草料，早起还有人叫早，夜里睡觉前还有人给打来洗脚水烫烫脚，以便解乏。而冬捕前的冰院子却与此完全不同。

等待，伙计们快来报到啦
Waiting and eager to get to work.

Many detailed preparations begin even before the winter fishing starts. First of all, people pour water onto the yard to turn it into an ice yard. The name ice yard derives from water courtyard, which refers to a kind of inn for large carts in the north. In the past, in places close to the Songhua, Yalu, Nenjiang and Tumen rivers, the roads became difficult to travel on when it snowed, but the frozen river surfaces became wide roads for carts and sledges. Especially before the Chinese new year, people from villages in the mountains and on the plains hitched their carts, loaded them with various specialties such as yellow tobacco, mushrooms, animal hides and furs, pine nuts, hazelnuts, pheasants, mountain rabbits, soybeans, miscellaneous grains, frozen fish, frozen tofu, starch noodles, etc., and drove the carts and sledges along the frozen rivers to markets in the cities, where they traded the specialties for sacrificial paper (burned for the departed), incenses, candies, kitchen soda, cloth materials, ready-made garments, bowls and chopsticks, candles, pictures of the Kitchen God, the Heaven God, the Earth God and the Door God, New Year pictures and other goods for the New Year, and then drove along these same roads back to their home villages to honor their ancestors and worship the gods. The fact that rivers froze over in the cold north and became smooth roads for carts and sledges gave birth to a business—the water courtyard, which functioned as a kind of horse and cart inn on ice. The water courtyard, in fact, was an ice yard, which was built on the riverside and received cart drivers who were transporting goods from inside and outside of the mountains in all directions. The ice yard cart inn was like an ordinary cart inn. It offered a warm big *kang* (bed-stove) and a variety of meals. Afterwards, the diners could enjoy a performance of the singing-dancing duet and folk dramas of the north. There were staff to feed horses with forage at night and provide morning calls. There were also people who brought warm water for travelers to wash and warm their feet before they went to bed to help them recover from fatigue. The ice yard in Chagan Nur in winter fishing season, however, is altogether a different matter.

查干淖尔冬捕前的冰院子是为了“鱼”。这里的鱼，就有如那些从四面八方归来的“车马客人”，这是为迎接它们而专设的一个“院子”。这里的冰院子，是名副其实的冰院子。在查干淖尔渔场，有一个一千米见方的大院子，四周是一间间巨大的房子。夏天，房门紧闭，冬捕的各种工具存放在里面，偌大的渔场院子便成了渔夫和家属在此织网、补网、晒网、晾网的好去处。而冬季，那些修理好准备拖到冰上去实施捕鱼的各类工具，都要先摆放在院子里，然后“分堆”。分堆就是分类。要按照每一个网队所使用的工具归堆。常规的渔猎工具也就几样，主要是船、网之类。可是北方查干淖尔的捕鱼工具却多到三十几样，这些工具90%左右是用来征服冰封雪冻的江河，所以可以称为“冰雪冬捕”。无论是凿冰的冰镩，还是三丈三长的“穿杆”；无论是舀冰的“冰崩子”，还是绞网的马轮子；还有在冰上“撮鱼”的“冰撮子”；在冰上固定马轮的“刨锛儿”，一切的一切，都是为了对付北方的严寒和厚厚的坚冰。在查干淖尔，捕鱼工具随着冬捕而诞生，连它们的名称都与冰与雪紧紧组连在一起。形态更是坚硬，结实，要准备与冰硬碰硬……

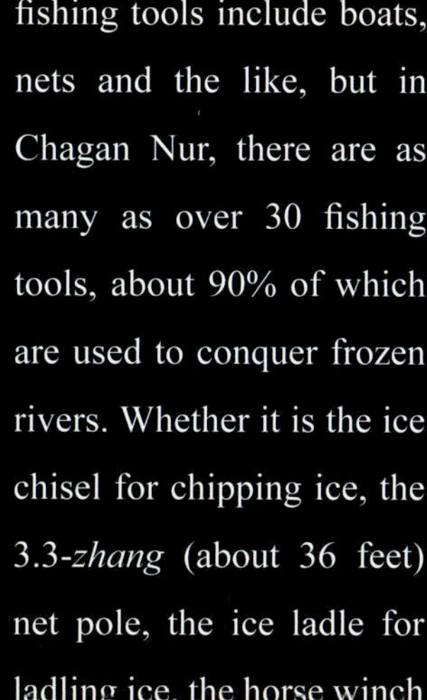

The ice yard of Chagan Nur prepared before the winter fishing is for fish. It is designed specifically to receive fish, just as the men and horses from thousands of miles away were received at the water courtyards. And it is an ice yard in the most literal sense. At the Chagan Nur fishing grounds, there is a huge courtyard of about 1000 square meters surrounded by huge houses. In summer, the doors are closed, with various winter fishing tools stored inside the houses; the huge yard is used by fishermen and their families for weaving, patching, sunning and airing fishing nets. In winter, the tools, repaired and ready for use, are placed in the yard first and then separated, or classified, into several heaps, each of which belongs to a certain team that will use the tools. Commonly seen fishing tools include boats, nets and the like, but in Chagan Nur, there are as many as over 30 fishing tools, about 90% of which are used to conquer frozen rivers. Whether it is the ice chisel for chipping ice, the 3.3-*zhang* (about 36 feet) net pole, the ice ladle for ladling ice, the horse winch for hauling fishing nets, the flat shovel for gathering fish on ice, or the ice pinch for fixing horse-drawn cart wheels on ice, everything is meant for dealing with the cold and the thick ice of the northern winter. In Chagan Nur, fishing tools were invented along with winter fishing, and even their names are closely linked to ice and snow. They are hard and sturdy, ready to meet the equally hard ice head on...

那些堆放在渔场院子里的工具，已经一件件经老渔夫老木匠的手修理好，就等着寒风刺骨的日子一到，大湖冰冻到一米多厚之时，便会在一夜之间被渔夫们拖出院子，进入到寒冷无比的厚厚冰原上去，施展各自用途去了。那时候，渔场的大院子里就会变得空空荡荡啦。空空荡荡的大院子，就要开始浇冰了。浇冰，是在院子里的地上洒水，让北方的严寒使水冻成亮晶晶的厚厚的冰层，俗称冰院子或冰场。

The tools piled in the fishing ground yard have been repaired piece by piece by the old fishermen and carpenters. They are waiting for the days of the biting cold, when the ice over the big lake is one meter thick. Then the tools will be hauled out of the yard overnight and moved onto the frigid and thick ice sheet, where they will be put to their respective uses. In the now empty courtyard, water will be poured onto the ground, where it will become frozen, forming a thick layer of ice—thus the name ice yard or ice ground.

其实，千百年来，北方的人就是在与冰与雪打交道。本来冬季的大地，经寒冬的风雪一吹，所有的一切都笼罩在冰雪之中，人们和动物，家禽出行不便，为何好好的院子，却还要浇水冻冰呢？许多人都在寻找查干淖尔的神奇和奥秘，而这冰院子就是它的神奇所在。

In fact, for thousands of years, the northerners have lived with ice and snow. In winter, everything is covered in ice and snow, already making it hard for people and animals to move about. Why then pour water that freezes on the ground in a perfectly fine courtyard? Many people seek to understand the wonders and mysteries of Chagan Nur, and the ice yard is where the magic lies.

冬季，当严寒在一眨眼间就把地表上的一切都冻硬，当万物皆因寒冷而瑟瑟，而此时却到了查干淖尔最欢乐的时日，他们要迎接鱼归仓。鱼归仓，就如秋天大地上的粮归仓，不是几条鱼而是成千上万吨的鱼一下子拉进院子，如何“对付”这些鱼？只有冰院了能胜任……

In winter, when the cold freezes everything on the ground in the blink of an eye, when all things cower in the cold, Chagan Nur ushers in its most joyful time. For this is when they bring in the fish, just as grains are brought into the granary in autumn. Yet they are not dealing with a few fish, but thousands of tons of fish that are hauled into the yard. What to do with all this fish? Only the ice yard is capable of the job...

冰院子浇冰要赶在严寒落雪之前动手，不要使雪落在地上，这样浇出的冰不是白冰。雪在冰层之下会与天颜色一致，晃眼睛，渔夫们不好干活。要在大雪还没

落下，选一个极其寒冷的日子，以扫帚扫净院子，然后开始洒水。洒水要从院子的一头开始以水龙头均匀地向地上喷水。旧时是以人挑水，以葫芦瓢舀水泼向院子。那水一泼出去，落地便已成冰。

Pouring water to create the ice yard must begin before the snow starts falling on the yard ground to ensure that the ice formed on the ground is white ice. If there is snow under the ice, it will reflect the color of the sky, making it more difficult to see and the fishermen's work harder. Therefore, before it snows, the people here will choose a very cold day, sweep the yard with brooms, and begin sprinkling and pouring water on it. The water pouring should begin from one end of the yard, using a hose to cover the ground evenly with water. In the past, people carried the water and poured water on the yard ground using a gourd ladle. The water became ice the moment it hit the ground.

一天一宿要浇六次。要等大约两袋烟的工夫，头一茬冰已冻平，才能浇第二遍。不能快，也不能慢。快了，头一茬冰会与下一茬连在一起，不能掌握冰的平均厚度；慢了，头一茬与下一茬容易起层，不利于冬季冰的使用。

The water pouring must be done six times within one day and one night. It takes around the time to smoke two pipes for the first layer of water to freeze evenly. Only then can the second pouring begin. It cannot be done too quickly or too slowly. If it is done too quickly, the first and second layers will stick together, which makes it harder to have evenly-spread ice; if it is done too slowly, the first ice and second ice may become layered, which is not conducive to the use of winter ice.

摄影 / 闫来锁
Photograph by / Yan Laisuo

查干淖尔渔场冬季的冰院子是冬捕的一个重要环节，作用非常重要。那冰要有半尺厚才行，要抗砸，抗磨损，因为每天要有成百上千吨的冻鱼从寒冷的冰面上拉进院子，一倒进院子，冻鱼便变成了“鱼山”。这时，冰院子里的渔夫就开始“炒鱼”了。炒鱼，就是挑选分类。要分清各种鱼，什么胖头、鳡条、草根、鲤鱼、大白鱼、青鱼，船丁子等等不同品种；还要分出大小。这种分工、挑选可忙坏了渔夫。

The ice yard is a critical link in winter fishing and serves an important function. The ice must be half a *chi* (around 15 centimeters) thick, and it must be able to withstand use and wear, for thousands of tons of fish will be transported from the frozen lake into the yard every day. Once there the fish are poured onto the ice, forming large piles of “fish mountains”. The fishermen in the ice yard will then begin to sort the fish, which means selecting and classifying the fish. The fish are classified by species that include the bighead carp, yellowcheek, grassroot, carp, big white fish, herring, whiting, etc., then classified based on their sizes. This sorting process can keep the fishermen quite busy.

那时，冰院子各仓库的大门已大敞四开，各类各种大小的鱼，该进哪个仓库，全靠在冰上滑运过去。还是在冰院子浇冰时，其实冰道已直通各个仓库里了，地表上的冰已直达仓库的墙根。鱼儿们直接可以滑动过去，又不伤着鱼肉。特别是浇好的冰院子，加上已落了薄薄的小雪，冰上面又滑又软，可以快速滑动鱼，又不磕碰鱼身，真是一个绝妙的“冬运”妙方。

At this time, the gates of the storages around the ice yard are wide open. All kinds of fish of varying sizes are slid directly to the appropriate storage. When the ice yard was made, ice lanes leading to the storages were also made. The ice extends all the way to the wall of the storages, so the fish can be slid straight into their storages without being damaged. Sometimes when a light snow has fallen, the ice surface becomes slippery and soft, and the fish can be transported quickly and smoothly—what an ingenious method of winter transportation.

那时，渔场的冰院子已沸腾了！

你看吧，那些负责滑鱼归类的人把鱼抱起，然后一抛，便把鱼分别“滑”进仓库里，那边“小打”（年轻的渔夫）们和在库里负责垛鱼的小伙计们，一个个的在严寒中早已甩掉了大皮袄，只穿着一件小褂，棉帽子的帽耳也卷翘起来，大汗淋漓地大喊一声：“三号库——！”

嗖——！咣当当——！

只听一阵巨响，一条鲜红粉嫩的大冻鱼便在冰院子的冰上滑了过去，直奔三号库！

又有人喊："躲开——！二号库——！"

又一阵响动，另一条冻鱼也滑过冰院子，迅速到达库房。而且，冻鱼相互各走各自的"线"，决不相撞。

By this time, the ice yard is bustling with activity and excitement.

Those responsible for the classification of the fish pick up the fish and toss it onto the ice lane leading to the storage, where young fishermen and workers responsible for piling fish in the storage have already removed their big leather coats, leaving on only light jackets despite the cold winter weather.With the flaps of their cotton-padded caps curled up, they call out loudly: "Storage 3!"

Whoosh! Clang!

There is a loud noise as a big frozen red fish is slid onto the ice, heading straight for Storage 3.

Someone else calls out: "Out of the away! Storage 2!"

With another flurry of sounds and movements, another frozen fish is slid across the ice, quickly reaching the storage. The best part is, the frozen fish each travel on their own route and never collide.

那时的查干淖尔渔场的冰院子，就像七月流火，溢光流彩。鲜鱼冻鱼裹带着荒野和大自然奇异的酷寒气息，各色鱼组成的五彩缤纷的色泽，在空气中和阳光下飞舞交叉，奇丽辉映，寒冷的空气中流动着欢乐。大片的冰鱼在地上滑动时交叉运走，从来没有碰撞和堵塞，那是一种技艺和智慧的运行，那是人类珍贵的生存遗产的杰作。

The Chagan Nur ice yard overflows with light and colors at this time. Fresh frozen fish, wrapped in the cold atmosphere of the wilderness and nature, glitter with various colors that dance and intersect in the air and the sunlight. In the resplendent brilliance, the cold air is filled with joy. Large masses of frozen fish are slid on the ground in a crisscrossing fashion, but there is never a collision or a "traffic jam". It is an operation carried out with skill and wisdom, a masterpiece of human heritage preserved.

随着鱼涌出冰面，北方的冰院子日夜在上演着冰雪滑鱼大戏。渔场那一间间偌大的库房里，转眼间，鲜鱼被一垛垛地堆码在一起，形成一道道奇丽无比的自然景观。在漆黑的夜里，院子里要点上马灯，或凭借着天上寒空的月色的光亮来运鱼滑鱼。那冻鱼砸在冰院子上并以极快速度滑动时，与天上的星光和院子里的马灯火亮，组合在一起，使渔场之夜辉煌灿烂，那是少有人完全知晓的文化去处。一种古老的自然文化气息在升腾着，随着寒风冷雪飘进久远的岁月里去了。查干淖尔，就这样以它的独特景观向世人展示着这个最后的渔猎部落的生动和完美。

As the fish are hauled out from the lake, the ice yard stages a grand drama of sliding fish over ice and snow that lasts from day into night. Before long, the storages are filled with stacked heaps of fresh fish to form an unparalleled scene from nature. To slide and transport the fish in the dark of the night, the yard is lit by lanterns or the moon that hangs in the cold sky. As the frozen fish smash onto the ice yard and slide swiftly across the icy ground, as the stars twinkle in the sky and the lantern burns bright in the yard, everything comes together to create a brilliant night on the fishing ground, where a northern culture that no one as yet fully understands still remains. An ancient natural and cultural atmosphere fills the air and drifts with the cold wind and dancing snowflakes into the long gone past. Through its unique landscape and its sights and sounds, Chagan Nur continues to display the richness and perfection of life in the world's last fishing tribe

Fishing on the Ice Lake

冰湖渔猎

马轮拉网，

这一网队又要迁徙走向远方。

所以人们常说，

查干淖尔的马，都是一些有灵气的马。

在查干淖尔，马，给人留下不少奇异的记忆，

但那些记忆都与冰、与雪有直接的关系，

或许查干淖尔马就是冰与雪的活态生命体。

查干淖尔马的灵气都在冰上、在雪上、在冰与雪的核心之中，

人们叫它查干淖尔马，

是生命与生命的对接。

The net has been pulled up by the horse-drawn winch,

and the team of net handlers is moving to another place.

People often say that the horses at Chagan Nur possess a spiritual aura.

In Chagan Nur, horses have left people with a number of curious memories,

but those memories are all directly related to ice and snow.

Perhaps Chagan Nur horses are the living embodiments of ice and snow.

The spiritual aura of Chagan Nur horses is contained

within the very core of the ice and snow.

Known as Chagan Nur horses,

they are human's closest ally.

生命托举的自然

Nature Held Up by Life

霜马渔歌之一
A Song of Frost and Horses

在世界范围内，用马轮子转动来拖拉大网，鱼儿跃出冰层，查干淖尔保留了这种原生态的生产方式，这其实是充满了人对生命的理解……

在这里，马是一种独特的生命。

每年，当第一片雪花飘落，当寒风渐渐吹干地上的草，吹落树上的叶子，查干淖尔的马儿就开始不安地躁动起来了。它们天天面对主人不停地刨地，并打着响鼻儿。仿佛在催促主人，快快行动吧，去捕

当马车在冰上奔跑时，那种激情一次次地感染着人，难道地球上的生命不是奇迹吗？它，就是不会说话，它如果会说话，主人一定会听到它在呵呵地乐呢，因为上冰干活的马，主人要喂它一顿鸡蛋黄。

As the horses turn the winch and pull up the big net, fish leap out from the ice—in all of the world, only Chagan Nur has retained this production method adapted to its original ecology, which in fact reflects a true understanding of life...

Every year, when the first snowflake falls, when the cold wind gradually dries up the grass on the ground and blows the leaves off the trees, Chagan Nur's horses become restless. Standing before their masters, they paw at the ground and let out loud snorts, as though urging their masters to hurry up, take action, and go fishing.

When the horse-drawn carts speed across the ice, the excitement is infectious. Isn't life on earth a miracle? The horse cannot talk. But if it does, its master will surely hear

马轮拉网，这一网队又要迁徙走向远方。所以人们常说，查干淖尔的马，都是一些有灵气的马。在查干淖尔，马，给人留下不少奇异的记忆，但那些记忆都与冰与雪有直接的关系，或许查干淖尔马就是冰与雪的活态生命体。查干淖尔马的灵气都在冰上、在雪上、在冰与雪的核心之中，人们叫它查干淖尔马，是生命与生命的对接。

The net has been pulled up by the horse-drawn winch, and the team of net handlers is moving to another place. People often say that the horses at Chagan Nur possess a spiritual aura. In Chagan Nur, horses have left people with a number of curious memories, but those memories are all directly related to ice and snow. Perhaps Chagan Nur horses are the living embodiments of ice and snow. The spiritual aura of Chagan Nur horses is contained within the very core of the ice and snow. Known as Chagan Nur horses, they are human’s closest ally.

冬捕，人要在冰原上不停地迁徙。脚和冰雪时时面对，去度过一冬天漫长的光阴。人和马，都要武装自己的脚。人，既是自己的“鞋匠”，又是给马挂掌的“铁匠”。当寒风扫来厚厚的积雪，人和马的脚上都长了“丁脚”（一种雪疙瘩）。于是巧手的渔夫们给自己绑上“扎什”，给马儿打上带翅膀的钉掌，给走冰带来了方便。冬天属于查干淖尔的智慧者，是他们挖掘出一种生存的本能，让人类巨大的创造力得到前所未有的释放。

AIRBORNE

摄影 / 闫来锁
Photograph by / Yan Laisuo

During winter fishing, the fishermen must keep moving on the ice, with their feet constantly in contact with the ice or snow; it is like this all through the long winter, so men and horses must arm their feet. Humans are their own shoemakers as well as blacksmiths who make the horseshoes. When cold winds sweep over and leave a blanket of deep snow here, both men and horses develop frostbite on their feet. So the skillful fishermen tie *zhashi* cloth on their feet and shod horses with winged horseshoes to facilitate their travel on the ice. Winter belongs to the wise people of Chagan Nur, who have tapped a survival instinct, releasing the enormous creative energy of humans.

那些凝固在冰中的气泡是冰的气息，大草原在冰雪下呼吸。马，毅然踏上冰面，它用铁蹄唤醒着千年的记忆，万年的沉睡，让一个民族醒来。那曾经是一个马背上的民族。马儿扬起飘荡的密鬃，让雪去擦亮每一根长鬃，再把失去召回。

The air bubbles trapped in the ice are the breath of the ice. The prairie breathes under the ice and snow. Horses set foot on the ice resolutely, and with their shod hooves they wake up memories that go back a thousand years, interrupt a deep slumber that has lasted even longer, and awaken an entire nation that used to live its life on the horseback. With their thick mane flying in the air, and the snow brightening their every hair, the horses embark on a path to bring back the lost past.

雪和霜，渐渐地凝固在它的皮毛上了……那些雪、霜，渐渐地打了卷儿，让奔驰的马儿的细毛变粗、变硬，升起热腾腾的气味儿。气味在茫茫的科尔沁草甸上飘荡，变成了冰冷的浓雾，或再生的霜粒，把马儿打扮成一个久远民族的雕像，动人地刻在了自然中。马儿欢奔，鬃儿成了毛笔，马儿成了书法家。我看见它在辛勤地写作。大地上的冰雪，正是一张洁白的宣纸，游牧民族的身影正在回归。我们不但听到马蹄奔驰敲打大地的回响，我们仿佛又看到了圣主成吉思汗的身影，他打马驰骋在白雪的牧原。冰和雪，糊住了北方的牧原。马群用力去敲打大地，让冰在土地上绽放。查干淖尔，真是冰雪游牧的赞歌。

Snow and frost have gradually encrusted the fine hair of the galloping horse, making its hair thicker and harder, while heat rises from its body. The hot air drifts across the vast Horqin Grassland, turning into a cold fog or frost particles, and the horse, thus adorned, becomes a poignant statue of the age-old nation, carved in nature. The horse gallops on; its mane bristles become a writing brush, and the horse becomes a calligrapher. I see it hard at work, writing. The ice and snow on the ground is a piece of white rice paper. The figures of the nomadic people are returning. Not only do we hear the reverberating sounds of running horse hooves beating on the ground, but we also seem to see the figure of the great Genghis Khan. He spurs his horse onward on the snow-white grassland. The northern grassland has been pasted with snow and ice. The herd of horses and their hooves gallop over the land, stepping down hard and making the ice bloom over the land. Chagan Nur is a hymn to the nomadic life in a world of ice and snow.

世界上，人有各种瘾，但在查干淖尔最大的瘾是打鱼，人在查干淖尔冬捕的冬日，一切寒冷、劳累、困乏，都已抛到九霄云外了。网房子厨房送来的一碗饺子、一碗豆包、一碗豆面卷子都含着无尽的香甜，让冷风和粮食一起吞进肚里。

There are all kinds of addiction in the world, but in Chagan Nur, the biggest addiction is fishing. In the winter fishing season, people there forget all about their cold and fatigue. A simple bowl of dumplings, steamed buns stuffed with sweetened be-an paste or bean flour rolls from the kitchen can taste endlessly delicious. It is gobbled up along with the cold wind.

家乡土烧锅（作坊）自酿的老酒带着乡情流进肠胃，烫热了查干淖尔渔夫的情怀。有的人，竟然几天几夜不下冰，茫茫的冰原，就是他们的家。几代人啦，都是在这样的环境里生存，他们生就了一副抗寒耐冷的性格，别土无有，别处不生。只有查干淖尔，最后的渔猎部落里来往着这样的汉子。

The home-brewed liquor from the *tushaoguo* (liquor workshop) flows into the stomach with thoughts of home and warms the hearts of the Chagan Nur fishermen. Some of them stay on the ice for days in a row. The vast ice field is their home. Generations of fishermen have survived in this environment and season. They are born with a resilience to the cold, which is found in no other place. Men like them are found only in the last fishing tribe of Chagan Nur.

在茫茫的查干淖尔冰面上捕鱼，旗和灯这两样是万万不可缺少的，这属于在冰面上作业必备的用具。冬季捕鱼是一项要行动一致的集体活动，拿什么放什么要靠渔把头来统一指挥，这就靠把头手里的旗和灯了。

Two things are absolutely indispensable when fishing on the ice in Chagan Nur: The flag and the lamp. They are essential tools for operations on the ice. Winter fishing is a collective effort that requires all participants to move in unison by following the command of the fishing master. The flag and the lamp are what he uses to signal orders.

冰面茫茫无际，渔把头手握一杆大旗坐在头一架爬犁上，他用自己的慧眼在泡子上选择打冰眼下网的窝子，一旦他选好合适的窝子，就会大喊一声："插旗！"立刻有人手举大旗，把旗插在冰面上，这叫"打范围"。打范围，就是按"旗"的方位来打。

On the endless expanse of ice, the fishing master sits on the front sledge, holding a big flag. With discerning eyes, he surveys the ice for the best sites to make the net-casting "eyes". Once he has selected a good spot, he calls out, "Flag!" and a man quickly plants the big flag on the ice. This is called "staking the range"; the ice eyes will later be made according to the location of the flags.

每一个冬捕的网队要有六杆大旗，九杆小旗，称为"翅旗"。当渔把头选好窝子时，他吩咐插旗的先在网窝子的四个角（长方形，两头长，中间宽）插上旗，剩下两杆，一杆插在下网眼处，一杆插在出网眼处。下网眼处，叫"下网旗"；出网眼处，叫"出网旗"。

Each of the winter fishing net teams has six big flags and another nine small flags known as "wing flags". When the fishing master has selected a site, he orders the man in charge of flag planting to plant the big flags at the four corners of the net site (a rectangle with two long ends and a wide middle). The fifth flag is placed at the net casting site and known as the net casting flag, while the final flag is planted at the net extraction site and known as the net extraction flag.

旗的颜色往往是红色，因为颜色鲜明。旗的作用是“指挥”下网出网的。在野外冰雪的湖面上，常常是冻雾升腾，大雪飞刮，有什么事需要招呼既听不清也看不清；但旗一摆，就知道“有情况”。旗有“旗语”，一有情况，摆大旗“发令”。下网大旗往左边晃，是告诉小股子提防左边；往右边晃，是注意右边冰下的情况。出网时，出网旗指挥跟网的和马轮子，也有一套“摆旗”的规矩和手法。这叫“旗指挥”，也叫旗语。执旗的人在冬捕时固定执旗；领网把头要时时注意旗帜，以便掌握运网情况。如果打网一点点拖到了“旗”换“灯”就叫“贪黑了”。贪黑作业时，白天的六面旗换成了六盏灯。

1 冰歌赞马（左1）

2 冰原神曲（右上2）

3 目光的投放（右下3）

1.A bird’s eye view (left)

2.Drawing on a canvas of ice (upper right)

3.An icy fishing ground (lower right)

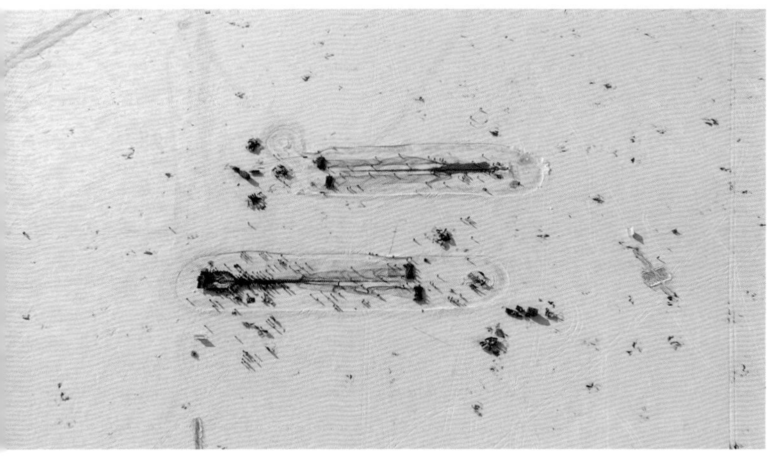

The color of the flag is often red because it is bright and easily visible. The role of the flag is to "command" the people engaged in casting and extracting the net. Frozen lake surfaces are often engulfed by heavy mist and whirling snowflakes, making it difficult for people to hear or see. However, a wave of the flag sends a clear signal that "something is up." Flags have a "language" of their own (more formally known as flag semaphore). When something comes up, a wave of the flag sends the order. When the net casting flag moves to the left, it tells the fishermen to pay attention to the left side; when it waves to the right, it is signaling them to pay attention to conditions beneath the ice on the right side. When the net is being pulled out, the people in charge of the extraction and the horse-drawn winch follow the signals of the net extraction flag, for which there is another set of rules governing how it is waved.During the winter fishing, the flag holder is responsible only for handling the flag. The fishing master leading the net operation must constantly watch the flag to stay on top of things. When the net operation is delayed so that the flag is replaced by the lamp, it is referred to as "working in the dark", in which case the six flags used during the day are replaced by six lamps.

灯又叫"风灯"。这是因为太阳一落山，冰面上风就起来了。冰上的灯都叫"风灯"，以防风而得名。风灯依旧挂在白天插旗的位置上。风灯的位置和白天插旗的位置一样，只不过风灯有了两样颜色，一红一绿。这红绿，也许是延续了古老颜色的意义。红，运网要立刻停，这是准有地方刮网、卡网什么的；绿，就是恢复正常作业，马轮继续。

The lamp is also called "wind lamp", because the wind starts to blow on the ice after sunset. All the lamps on ice are called wind lamps because they must be windproof. The wind lamps are held by the fishing master and placed at the same locations where the flags were planted during the day. The difference is that the wind lamp has two colors, red and green. What the colors signal may have been inherited from ancient meanings given to these colors. Red means to immediately stop operating the net,

indicating that the net must be scraping against something or is stuck; green means to resume normal operations and for the winch to continue hauling the net.

风灯是用铁壳子做的那种马灯一样的灯，从前也有用木制四框的老马灯，上带盖，防雨又防风。变换颜色是用红或绿布子来蒙在灯口处，以告之对方。这执管“旗”和“灯”的人是大工，由总把头负责或指派专人。在查干淖尔，这种灯又叫“气死风”，是说只要这盏灯在冰天雪地里一亮，老北风也拿它没办法，这其实是渔民对自己在冰天雪地里劳作的歌颂。

The wind lamp is made of iron sheet and resembles barn lanterns. In the past, there was a kind of four-frame lantern made of wood, which had a cover on top to keep out the rain and wind. Changing the color of the wind lamp was achieved by covering the burner with a red or green cloth. The person in charge of the flags and lamps must be an experienced worker, and is usually the general fishing master or someone appointed by him. In Chagan Nur, this lamp is also known as “driving the wind mad”, meaning that once it has been lit, even the strong northerly wind can do nothing to it. The name can in fact be seen as reflecting the pride that the fishermen take in braving the ice and snow to work.

在冰天雪地里捕捞，首先得用手，“手闷子”很重要。手闷子，就是手套。在查干淖尔，冬捕的渔民都喜欢戴四个指头合并在一起，大拇指单在一个套里的手闷子。四个指头放在一起，可以保存热量，做时又省工省时。

马背霜丛
Frost Bush on Horse Back

天堂
Paradise

When fishing on the ice, hands are paramount, which makes gloves very important. In Chagan Nur, the winter fishermen like to wear mittens, with one section that covers the thumb and another section that covers all four fingers. Mittens help the four fingers that are in the same section stay warm and are convenient for work.

渔民多穿皮袄。老皮袄又称老皮筒子、皮壳子。这是用整张羊皮制作的，毛朝里，让皮子露在外，腰上扎腰带子。老皮袄都是打鱼的从镇上皮铺买来的。每到秋天，皮匠们就从来自草原上的皮货商或牧民手中收购大量的皮张，然后熟制。熟皮制衣是一道古老的手艺。皮匠们戴着一条长长的拖地的皮围裙，整天在臭烘烘的作坊里忙乎着。这种熟好的皮张，柔软厚实，做成皮袄很是防风抗寒。每年渔民都要从镇里的皮铺拉回大量的皮袄，穿上它上冰。

Most of the fishermen wear sheepskin jackets, which are also known as old leather jackets, leather shells, etc. It is made with a whole sheepskin, with the fleece on the inside and the skin on the outside, and fastened with a waist belt. The sheepskin jackets are bought from leather-fur shops in town. Every autumn, leather tanners purchase a large amount of leather and fur from furriers or herdsmen and tan them. Tanning leather to make clothing is an ancient craft. The leather tanner wears a full-length leather apron and busies himself in the foul-smelling workshop all day long. The tanned hides are soft and thick. Jackets made of them are wind-proof and cold-resistant. Each year, fishermen bring back a large number of such jackets from the leather-fur shops in town and wear them on the ice.

冬天在茫茫的风雪中穿上这种老羊皮袄，打鱼人会显得分外的威风和有精神头，而且这种皮袄领口和袖口开阔，也便于头和手活动，是一种渔民十分喜爱的穿戴。冬天到查干淖尔来的人都想穿上一件老羊皮袄到冰上去，或者纯粹为了体会这种渔猎文化。

In the wind and snow of winter, the fishermen strike a particularly imposing and spirited figure in their sheepskin jackets.The jacket has an open collar and cuffs, which allows for easy head and hand movements, and is much favored by fishermen. All the visitors to Chagan Nur in the winter want a sheepskin jacket that they can wear on the ice, perhaps simply to better experience this fishing culture.

渔民们家家都有这东西。从柜子里、仓子里拿出一件，穿上去照一张相，那浸泡着查干淖尔潮湿鱼草气息的老皮袄十分沧桑神圣。有时，我们简直不敢相信自己的耳朵，风灯这名，只能来自查干淖尔打鱼部落。

Every fishing family has at least one of these jackets. Take one from the wardrobe or the cabinet, put it on and take a picture, and notice how the jacket, long steeped in the moist smell of fish and grass at Chagan Nur, has a time-worn and almost sacred look. And then there are times when we almost cannot believe our ears. Take the name “wind lamp”, it could only have come from Chagan Nur.

兵马冰屋冰雪图

Horses and Shed on the Ice

“牛皮绑”，其实就是一块皮子的别称。这块皮子相当柔软，在冰上捕鱼时一定要穿上，并可用来防止鱼扎脚。这种牛皮绑，也是渔民们自己熟的。而牛皮绑里往往要套上“水袜子”来取暖并暖和脚趾，这种水袜子防潮、防水又保暖。水袜子是一种棉线织的厚袜子，在江河湖泊边上作业的渔民，一年四季都离不了这种水袜子，因牛皮绑在外边兜着，这样多大多厚的袜子也就不显得笨重了，里边穿上水袜子，脚趾头可以自由伸动，便于拿土站稳。

Cattlehide gaiter. In fact, this simply refers to a piece of leather. The leather is quite soft and must be worn while fishing on the ice. It can prevent the feet from being cut by the fish. This cattlehide gaiter is also tanned by the fishermen themselves. “Water socks” must be worn beneath the cattlehide to keep the toes warm and nimble. The water socks are moisture-proof, waterproof and warm. The water socks are thick cotton socks, but thanks to the cattlehide gaiter on the outside, they do not seem bulky and clumsy. The water socks on the inside allow the toes to stretch freely, so they can hold on to the ground and maintain balance.

冰上和雪地里的活，全都是冰冷和打滑的，要稳定身体，全靠脚的力量，脚不稳则全身晃，使不上力气。而平底的牛皮绑配上软软的水袜子，正好适合冬捕时渔民使用。

Working on snow and ice is always cold and slippery. To maintain balance, the fishermen must rely on the strength of their feet; if the feet are unsteady, then the whole body sways, making it difficult to exert strength. The flat cattlehide gaiters, together with the soft water socks, is the perfect combination for fishermen during winter fishing.

打鱼的，一定要有一条“缠腰布子”。就像西北黄土高原上的人要有一条白羊肚手巾一样，东北的渔民要靠这缠腰布子来象征自己的职业特征。缠腰布子就是一般的白花旗布染成黑色或蓝色的布，镇子里的布店或乡下的染坊都有。一条缠腰布子要十米长，得可腰缠，一下子可缠个十道二十道的，这样起到壮腰保暖的作用。

A fisherman must have a waist cloth. Just like everyone who lives on the Loess Plateau in Northwest China must have a white “sheep-belly” towel, so every fisherman in Northeast China depends on the waist cloth to symbolize his profession. The waist cloth is simply an ordinary piece of white cloth dyed black or blue, available at the cloth shops in town or rural dyehouses. A waist cloth must be at least 10 meters in length, long enough to be wrapped around the midriff ten to twenty times in order to have the effect of protecting the waist and keeping it warm.

冰马、冰车和冰网垛图
Horses, Cart and Net Pile on the Ice

冬捕打网和上冰的渔民，人和冰水打交道，别说水往身上落，就是“气”也冷。这种“气”，指“冰气”。冰气从冰上起，吸人身上的热量。而人干活时付出热量，就容易出汗，一出汗，就容易受风。特别是腰部如受了风，人就无法再站立，于是人们就想到了使用缠腰布子来保护自己。因此，缠腰布子是打鱼人的一宝。

Fishermen casting nets on ice in winter deal with icy cold water. Even the vapor is cold, not to mention the water that splashes onto them. The vapor refers to “ice vapor”, which rises from the ice and takes heat away from human bodies. The fishermen expend calories and perspire when they work, which makes them susceptible to the cold wind. In particular, when their lower back suffers from the cold wind, it can make it impossible for them to stand straight. So they came up with a way of protecting themselves by wrapping a cloth around their waist. The waist cloth is one of the fisherman’s most important possessions.

缠腰布子多是冰上捕鱼渔民所用，而围脖巾也是冬捕时打冬网的渔民所用。这是一块长方形或三角形的蓝麻花布子，有时扎在腰上，起到了腰带子的作用，可以使皮袄紧紧地贴在肚子上和身上，有时风大，冰水四溅，就把这种布子扎在脖子上，并把一角一掀，盖住头，包住顶，免受冰水冷风的袭击。

Just as the waist cloth is used mostly by ice fishermen, so too the scarf is used by them. This is a rectangular or triangular piece of blue hemp fabric. Sometimes it is tied around the waist, functioning as a belt to keep the sheepskin jacket snug against the stomach and around the body. When it is windy and the icy water splatters, the cloth is tied around the neck, and a corner is lifted to cover the top of the head from the onslaught of the icy water and cold wind.

北方的冬天，捕鱼人的帽子非常重要，因为这儿太冷，帽子要不抗风，人就会冻麻。这里的捕鱼人爱戴的是貉壳帽子。貉是北方平原靠岗近水边的一种小动物，喜欢在江边柳丛一带奔走，它的皮毛特别的珍贵，主要是毛细密，根部柔软，毛发直长，特别抗风遮寒。

In the northern winter, hats are also important for the fishermen. Because of the extreme cold here, if a hat cannot ward off winds, it could cause the wearer to be frozen numb. The fishermen here prefer hats made of raccoon dog fur. The raccoon dog is a small animal that lives near hills and waters on the northern plains and can often be found in willow bushes along rivers. Its fur is prized for its fine and dense hair, which is long and straight with soft roots and especially good for protection against the wind and cold.

在查干淖尔一带，冬天如果谁能戴上一顶貉壳帽子，那是让人羡慕的事情。而渔把头，必须要戴上一顶貉壳帽子，这是他的威严。在冰上捕鱼，冷风最爱吹扫后脖子，脖子一受风，就会红肿，人便会缺氧头发昏，就会站不住。而貉壳帽子的毛正好可以挡住吹脖风，保住这关键部位不受寒。好的貉壳帽子还会“吃雾”，雪花落上，一抖就掉；风一过，老雪又会从帽子上的软毛上飘走，真是神奇的帽子。

In the Chagan Nur region, a raccoon dog fur hat is something to be envied in the winter. For the fishing master, wearing a raccoon dog fur hat is a must, as it is a symbol of his authority. While fishing on ice, the back of the neck is the most susceptible to attacks from the cold wind. This can cause the neck to become red and swollen, leading to hypoxia and dizziness and making it difficult for the victim to remain standing. The hair of the raccoon dog fur hat can block the wind blowing across the neck to protect this important body part from the cold. A good raccoon dog fur hat can even "eat fog", and snowflakes that fall on it are easily shaken off. When a wind blows over, the remaining snow will drift off from the soft hair of the hat. It truly is a wonderful hat.

渔民的鞋，叫“靰鞡头”。靰鞡是东北民间用牛皮做成的一种鞋。康熙三十七年（1698年）皇帝与皇太后第三次东巡，取道塞外，“九月壬申，上次克尔苏，临科尔沁故亲王满珠习礼墓前酹酒，孝庄皇后之父也。”（《清史稿·康熙本纪》）在满珠习礼墓前酹酒时，看到这里百姓脚上用一张动物皮裹着，康熙帝问：“这是什么？”百姓答：“鞋。”康熙是位聪明的帝王，他说：“此鞋独到奇特，又备受边民喜爱，既然没有名就叫它乌拉鞋吧！”这一下，这种鞋可就出了名了。因乌拉是地名，而靰鞡是皮革所制，所以后来以“靰鞡”来为名。查干淖尔捕鱼人喜爱靰鞡，就像喜欢自己的儿女一样。打鱼的人常说，冬天在冰上打鱼，只要脚不冻，人身就不易做病，而最好的保护脚的服饰就是靰鞡了。

The fishermen wear shoes that are called *wulatou*. The *wula* is a shoe made of cattlehide and worn in Northeast China. In the 37th year of Kangxi's reign (1698), the emperor, accompanied by the Emperor Mother, went on his 3rd eastern inspection tour by way of the regions beyond the Great Wall. "On the *renshen* day of September, the emperor went to Ke'ersu, where he visited the tomb of the late Prince Manzhuxili of Khorchin, and performed a libation. The tomb was that of Empress Xiaozhuang's father." (See "Biographic Sketches of Kangxi" in the *Draft History of Qing*.) During the libation, Kangxi noticed that the people were wearing animal skin around their feet, so the emperor asked, "What is that?" "Shoes," replied the people. A quick thinker, Kangxi remarked, "These shoes are unique, peculiar and much loved by the border people. Since it has no name, let's call it *wula*!" From then on, the *wula*'s name traveled far and wide. As the original characters that Kangxi used to name the *wula* were the same characters for an existing place name (乌拉), and because the *wula* shoes were made of leather, the shoes were later renamed with two different characters (靰鞡)that sound the same as *wula*, but contain the radical that means animal hide. The Chagan Nur fishermen love their *wula* as they love their own children. As the fishermen's saying goes, when fishing on the ice, as long as you keep your feet warm, you are not likely to fall sick, and nothing beats the *wula* when it comes to keeping your feet warm.

1 亲吻北方严冬

2 眺望心上的雪原

3 雪原冰水喝一口，关东大地任我走

（左上1；左下2；右3）

1.A Frigid Kiss (upper left)

2.An Icy View (lower left)

3.ASnowy Drink (right)

乌力格尔与渔夫
Mongolian Story Tellers and the Fishermen

在查干淖尔，冬天的冰面就是一场梦幻动漫，冰眼是雕刻在茫茫冰面上的原始符号。如果从飞机上或从四周的高坡上向冰面上鸟瞰，凿完的冰眼就像一条巨大的多腿苍龙伏卧在冰面上，前边的出网眼是它昂起的头，后边下网眼飘荡的旗是它的尾，而两旁排列整齐的396个小冰眼恰似它的无数条劲腿，使它移向远方。

In Chagan Nur, the ice surface in the winter is a scene from a fantastic anime. The ice eyes are primitive symbols carved on the icy expanse. If you take a bird's eye view from an airplane or from the surrounding high hills, you will see that the chiseled ice eyes seem to form a huge multi-legged dragon crouching on the ice. The net extraction eyes in the front form its raised head; the flags fluttering at the net extraction eyes constitute its tail; and the 396 small ice eyes arranged neatly on either side resemble the innumerable legs that propel the dragon forward.

这是一张印烙在人类历史年轮上的巨幅图画，而“作者”就是巧手的查干淖尔渔夫。接下来，渔夫们就要装饰这幅图画了。装饰，就是让自己走进图画中。

This is a vast drawing imprinted on the annual rings of human history, and the “painters” are the skilled Chagan Nur fishermen. Next, the fishermen will adorn the drawing—by walking into it.

过去打鱼的人是用“小股子”拖网拉网，但由于劳动量太大，于是后来改用马来拖拉了。马轮子的上轮盘处有“插眼”，便于插“轮杠”来套马。一个轮盘处可安四到五个轮杠，也就是说最多能套四五匹马。这主要是看网中鱼的多少和重量来定。马轮子现在一律使用金属的材料来制作，架子和爬犁都是铁的，而从前完全是木制马轮子。木制的马轮子由部落里的木匠来打制，往往选用榆木、柞木、色木、桦木等硬质的木材来打制。马轮子架子庞大，沉重，但是在冰上被马拖拉着却显得轻快。

In the past, fishermen used the “small wheel” to pull the net. However, because the task is so labor intensive, the small wheel was replaced by the horse-drawn winch. The wheel on top of the winch drum has “plug holes” for “wheel bars”, which are used to hitch the horses. One wheel can accommodate four to five “wheel bars”, which means up to four or five horses can be hitched to it. The number of horses used depends mainly on the quantity and weight of the catch. All the horse winches today are made of metal materials, with the frame and sledge made of iron. In the past, the winches were made entirely out of wood by carpenters in the tribal community, who often used elm, oak, painted maple, birch and other hard wood. The horse winch frame is bulky and heavy, but seem light when pulled by the horses on ice.

马轮子是冬捕的重大工具，也算较大的家伙。当网队上冰出发，那巨大的马轮子被马拖着在冰上飞奔很威风。而像样的马轮子是渔猎部落老手艺人的拿手工艺，他能把马轮子做得古朴、结实而好看。马轮子被人称为冰上钢琴，每当捕鱼开始，马轮发出“吱吱扭扭”的响声，加上赶马轮子的人的吆喝声和马轮手鞭花在空中炸响声，组成一种奇妙的冬捕交响乐，在寒冷的查干淖尔茫茫原野上飘荡着，给人带来无尽的神奇和欢乐。

The horse winch is an important tool and one of the larger gears used during winter fishing. When the net team sets out on the ice, the huge winch, pulled swiftly along by horses, can look quite imposing. A good horse winch is the pride of the old craftsman in the fishing tribe. He can produce winches that are simple, sturdy and pleasing

出鱼时的呐喊
A Joyous Call as the Fish are Hauled In

to look at. The winch is known as the piano on the ice; whenever the fishing begins, the winch sends out creaking sounds, which, together with the cries of the winch operator and whip cracks in the air, form a wonderful winter fishing symphony that reverberates across the vast and cold wilderness of Chagan Nur, bringing a sense of wonder and joy to the people.

鱼出冰，就像秋天农人收割庄稼。出网眼是一个三角形的大眼，它的大小根据鱼的多少大小随时来决定，一般是长四尺左右，宽三尺左右。随着马轮子拉着大绦，网缓缓地被拉出冰面。网两侧的小股子各人抄起不同的工具。有使大钩子的，主要是搭网“吃重”（承受力大）的地方；有使小钩子的，也叫“小套子”，他们时时地搭起冰上刚出水的网，往马轮子一方“送”。随着一声“回绦”的高喊声，这时要“打卡”。“打卡”说明一拉网已经完全出水了。卡，是一种叫“卡勾”的东西。它的作用是把网和绦卡好，以便小套子们松开后不往回拖。马轮子上一“打卡”，小套子们就回去重新再拖下一拉网。这个时候，出网口处是最幸福和有趣的地方了。随着网缓缓出冰，一群一群的银色大鱼争先恐后地翻出冰眼，领网的指挥出网口的小股子手使“抄捞子”和“鱼叉”不断地舀鱼和叉鱼。有时一抄子能抄起两三条大鱼，往上一扬，鱼在空中不断扭动，落在冰上又上下跳蹦，带起的水点在空中结成冰粒，掉在冰上像银豆一样闪光，真是精彩极了……

Getting the fish out from under the ice is just like farmers harvesting crops in autumn. The net extraction eye is a big, triangular opening. Its dimensions are subject at any time to the number and size of the fish, but is usually about four *chi* (1.2 meters) long and three *chi* (90 centimeters) wide. As the horse winch pulls the large braid, the net comes slowly out of the ice hole, and the small-share workers on either side of the net pick up their tools. Some use big hooks to help pull the "heavy" parts of the net (where the weight of the fish is); some use small hooks, also known as "small snares". They hook the net that has just come out of the water and send it in the direction of the winch. With a loud shout of "braid is back", it is time to "fix the hook", which signals that a net has completely cleared the water. The hook in "fix the hook" refers to a snap hook,the function of which is to fix the net and the braid rope so that they do not fall back into the water when the workers let go. Once the hook has been fixed, the workers go back to haul up another net. This is a time of joy and excitement at the net extraction hole. When the net comes slowly out of the ice, large numbers of big, silvery fish scramble and leap out of the ice eye. The fishing master commands the workers around the extraction hole to use the "ladles" and "fishing forks" to ladle or lift the fish. Sometimes, one move of the ladle can scoop up two or three big fish. One toss of the ladle sends the fish up into the air, where they twist and turn, before landing on the ice, where they continue to thrash up and down. The water drops that follow them freeze in midair and land on the ice as ice particles, glittering like silvery beans. It is truly a sight to behold...

而小股子们则开始“装网垛网”，这也可称为“供网”，就是把打完鱼的大网一层一层地好好地码起来，一搭子一搭子地叠好，恭恭敬敬地递给下一个

冰眼处，或垛在一旁的大车或爬犁上，准备拉向下一个网窝子。供，既是供给，又是一种深深的虔诚恭敬。

Now the "small-share" workers start to "fold and stack the net", which can also be called "providing the net". This refers to folding the big net that was just used for fishing into neat layers and delivering it to the next ice eye respectfully, or stacking it on a cart or sledge to be pulled to the next spot. Providing means to provide the net to the next site, as well as to provide the net with the deepest respect.

抽上一口关东烟，解累解馋解心宽

A smoke of Guandong tobacco to satisfy a craving and relieve fatigue

一到了冬天，查干淖尔处处充满了传奇，每一个小股子、渔把头、看网房子的都处在产生传奇和进入传奇的角色中，这是因为冬捕是人类和大自然的一场独特的搏斗。生活的每一个角落，都被冰镩击冰和马儿拖拉马轮子绞网的声响调动起来，那是生活和大自然的神经。当若千年过去之后，这些被岁月磨洗过的故事和传奇依然会精彩无比。

Chagan Nur turns into a place of legends in winter. Every small fisherman, the fishing master and the people watching the net sheds are creating legends and playing a part in those legends, for winter fishing is a unique struggle between humans and nature. Every corner of life is mobilized by the sounds of chiseling ice and horse winches turning. They are part of the nervous system of life and nature. Years from now, these stories and legends, polished by time,will still shine as they do now.

在这个地方，如果鱼不丰富，部落人便会遇到饥饿和贫困，人们早已意识到这种规律，于是这里就有了生活中主动地歌颂冰鱼的存在和冰雪的丰饶。鱼的形态的出现其实不单源于查干淖尔，在中国传统文化之中鱼是同“余”（剩余，富裕）观念连在一起的，这是人类借物和音来表述人的希望和追求。在出鱼的查干淖尔，鱼的文化体现得更加细微和普遍。每至年节或一些民俗日，人们便扭起了“鱼灯”秧歌，这是一种普遍传承与特殊传承的融合。在这儿，许多渔夫会扎“鱼灯”并熟悉鱼文化艺术。

1 渔猎战阵

2 拖网布阵

3 网山的托举

（左1；右上2；右下3）

1.Battle Formation for Fishing (left)

2.Laying out the Net Array (upper right)

3.Atop the Net Mountain (Lower right)

In Chagan Nur, if the fish fail to bring abundance to the communities, hunger and poverty ensue, a rule that the people have come to realize.And so singing praises for the ice fish and the bountiful snow and ice has become part of life here. Chagan Nur is not the only place where fish have special significance. The Chinese character for fish is homophonous with the character that means "surplus", therefore, in traditional Chinese culture, fish is associated with the idea of abundance, a case of people borrowing from something else to express their hopes and aspirations. In Chagan Nur, a place teeming with fish, the culture of fish is played out with even more subtleties and pervasiveness. During every New Year and certain folk holidays, the people here dance the fish lantern *yangge* (a rural folk dance), blending a common heritage with a specific heritage. Many fishermen can make their own fish lanterns and are familiar with the culture and arts associated with fish.

在查干淖尔，百姓一年四季是以“鱼”来过日子的。这儿，冬天捕来的鱼吃不完，就将其晒成干，挂在自家的房前屋后，表述着一个渔猎之地的风情风貌。而且，手艺巧的人还自己“扎鱼”，那是一种传统手艺。把草原上的庄稼秆（高粱、玉米或葵花秆）垛齐，然后用麻绳勒上，制成鱼的骨架，再用绸布（有红、黄等颜色）粘贴在上面，“鱼”就成了。

The inhabitants of Chagan Nur depend on fish for a living throughout the year. The winter fish that are not eaten are dried in the sun and hung in front of and behind houses, a scenic expression of a fishing community. The more artful members of the community know how to "bound" fish, which is a traditional handicraft. They gather crop stems from the grassland (sorghum, corn or sunflower stalks) and chop them to the same length, then bound them with hemp ropes to make the frame of the fish.Then they paste a silk cloth (red, yellow or some other color) over the frame and voila, a fish is born.

查干淖尔部落是鱼的世界。在这里，无论春夏秋冬，往村里的任何一个角落望去，都有“鱼”映入眼帘。两棵大树间拉过一条绳子，鱼串在上面风干。风吹来，那一串串的鱼干十分有韵味。而且，站在这些树下，一股浓浓的鱼的气息就从天上飘荡下来了。各家院子的墙上，也挂着各种鱼。鱼肉红红的，鲜鲜的，但已干透，可以随时带着走向远方。

The Chagan Nur tribal village is a world of fish. Here, regardless of the season, in any corner you look, there is fish. Between two big trees is a rope on which strings of fish have been hung to be air-dried. When the wind blows, the swaying strings of fish make for a pleasant sight. Standing beneath the trees, one catches a strong smell of fish wafting down from above. All kinds of fish hang on the walls of courtyards. The fish meat is red, fresh,but thoroughly dried, ready to be brought along by the traveler who journeys afar.

冬季，人家的苇墙上、房檐上，都有冻鱼挂在那里。那是一些鲜鱼，是以自然的寒冷保存着它们的新鲜和本色。这种冻鱼很是好吃，一点也不走味儿。

扎鱼灯是查干淖尔人的绝活。如果是大鱼灯，就要组合。往往头是一组，腰身是两组，尾是一组。肚腔里装灯烛，点燃后舞耍……

做这种鱼灯往往是大胖头鱼样，因这种鱼典型又形象。鱼身是红色，给人以透明的感觉，鱼翅用黄色，尾用浅红或粉色，表示它活泼逼真。而且，鱼的嘴还要会动。这种鱼灯被称为“活”物。用时人举着，上下一舞，那鱼嘴便会上下咬合，与真的鱼儿一般。

In winter, people hang frozen fish on their reed walls and eaves. These are fresh fish, their freshness and original quality preserved naturally by the cold. This kind of frozen fish is delicious, having lost none of its authentic taste.

Making fish lanterns is a unique skill of the Chagan Nur people. Big fish lanterns are a combination of parts. Often the head is a part; the body is two parts; and the tail is another part. Inside the fish belly are lights or candles, which are lit and carried in dances...

This type of fish lantern often takes the shape of the bighead carp, which is both representative of Chagan Nur and distinctive looking. The fish body is in red, which gives the impression of translucence. The fins are in yellow, and the tail is in light red or pink, to show that it is vivid and life-like. Moreover, the fish mouth moves. This kind of fish lantern is called a “living” thing; the mouth opens and closes as the lantern is raised and lowered by the people holding it.

渔猎的查干淖尔

Another Day of Fishing at Chagan Nur

摄影 / 刘玉忱
Photograph by / Liu Yuchen

在查干淖尔，一到冬季节令，这种鱼灯就更加受欢迎。特别是每年的腊月三十和正月十五的灯节，如果没有鱼灯出现是不行的。这是生活中的鱼和文化中的鱼的相互存在，一种更加鲜活的存在。而且，家家不但准备鱼灯，还要做冰灯。

The fish lantern is even more popular in the winter, and practically indispensable on Chinese New Year Eve and the Lantern Festival on January 15th of the lunar calendar. This marks the coexistence of the fish in everyday life and the fish in the cultural tradition, making both more vividly present. In addition to the fish lanterns, families also make ice lanterns.

冰灯是那种“鱼”文化的延续，是冬捕和冬季渔猎文化的印迹。人们做冰灯已十分熟练。一般是用木桶或挑水用的柳罐斗子、水筲等，盛上水，搬到户外。由于东北处于严寒地带，只一袋烟的工夫（大约十五分钟左右），器物中的水贴近边缘便上冻了。人们把器物中的水倒出，贴在器物上的“壳”就成了灯型。这时，人要会“取壳”。取壳，就是把冰套顺利地从器物中倒下来。往往是搬进屋内，在炕上或灶前一烤，冰壳会自动脱落，再及时将这些冰壳搬到户外，保持在寒冷环境里。这就是冰灯。用时，在灯心上点蜡烛，一盏盏晶莹的冰灯便做成了。它们把冰湖渔猎的生活照得通亮，让人们深深地记住了这个地方……

The ice lantern is an extension of the culture of fish and an imprint of the winter fishing culture. The people here are skilled at making ice lanterns. Buckets,willow baskets or bamboo pails are filled with water and moved outdoors. In the frigid winter climate of Northeast China, a mere15 minutes (about the time it takes to smoke a pipe) is enough for the water close to the walls of the containers to freeze.

摄影 / 闫来锁
Photograph by / Yan Laisuo

The water is then poured out from the containers, and the ice "shells" that have formed along the containers become the lantern frames. Then comes the "shell retrieval", which means removing the lantern frames from the containers. This is done easily by moving the containers indoors and heating them with the bed-stove or kitchen stove, which causes the ice shells to slip out from the containers. Once out of the containers, the ice shells must be immediately brought outdoors again and kept in the cold. These are the ice lanterns. When candles are lit in the hollow middle of the lanterns, the translucent ice glistens and illuminates the life in the fishing village, creating an indelible memory in people's hearts...

把网丝梳理成太阳的光芒
Sunshine through the Fishing Net

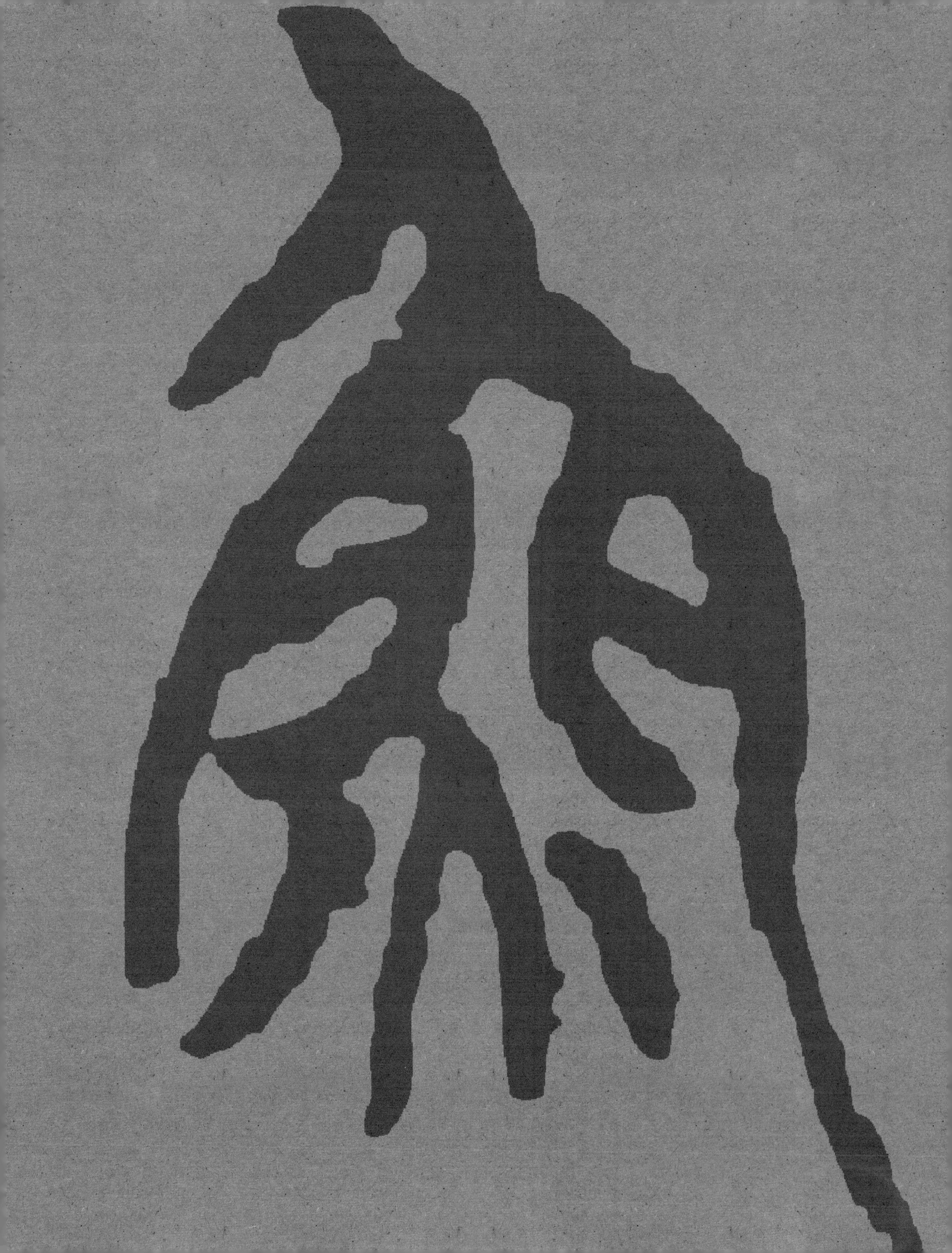

Passing the Torch

岁月传承

查干淖尔，

处处充满了传承。

人的一言一行，

一举一动，

都受到一种严格的心理制约。

他们懂得如何打鱼，

因为这里传承和弥漫着一种优秀的文化氛围。

Chagan Nur is a place filled with traditions.

These traditions have conditioned people's every word,

every deed and every move .

They know how to fish

because of the cultural environment that they have

inherited and is all pervasive here.

青年与一把搭勾
Youth and A Hook

渔猎岁月，最终把一个个小股子磨洗成渔把头。

Years of fishing on the ice finally turns the small-share workers into fishing masters.

多少次的生死使他们领略了查干淖尔的壮丽，终于让生命放射出奇异的光芒。查干淖尔是生命与生命真诚的碰撞，这是因为把头与徒弟都在接受岁月的磨洗。查干淖尔渔猎部落完整地保留着人类生存的一个过程，这是一种独立运行的过程，它仿佛是专为渔猎活动而生成的。

After living on the edge of life and death for so long, they have come to appreciate the magnificence of Chagan Nur and now their lives shine with a strange and beautiful glow. Chagan Nur is where lives cross paths and interact honestly, where both the fishing masters and their apprentices undergo the test of time. The Chagan Nur fishing tribe has preserved a process in the course of human survival, a process that operates independently, as though it was specifically created for the act of fishing.

把头，又叫渔把头，他是冬捕的领头人。渔把头是捕鱼人的主心骨，特别是冬捕，他要从一开始就被人心中默认他能带领这伙人打着鱼。首先是看把头的人品，有德行、有能力，并公认是“好人”、能干才行，他是冰上的灵魂人物。这就要求渔把头首先要精通选网窝子的本领，这是极其神奇的本领。

摄影 / 张军
Photograph by / Zhang Jun

最老最老的巴特尔
The Oldest Hero

抽上一口关东烟，遥望关东大雪原
Smoking a Guandong cigarette while looking out at the vast snow field of Guandong.

The master, also called the fishing master, is the leader of winter fishing operations. The fishing master is the backbone of the fishing crew, especially when fishing on the ice; he must be someone that people tacitly agree can lead the group. Character is first and foremost; the master must be virtuous, able and universally recognized as a "good man". He is the key person on the ice. This requires him to be skilled at choosing the location to cast the net, which is an extraordinary skill.

俗话说把头要会“识冰”。识冰，就是会看冰的颜色。冬季，鱼群在冰下喜欢成群地聚集在一块儿。由于鱼的聚堆往往使水涌动，冰面上的雪便微微起鼓，这种冰面是有鱼群的征兆。接下来是看颜色。有鱼群的冰层上往往结有数个气泡，气泡密集的方向是鱼群游动的方位，这样的冰层颜色发灰。还有就是会听冰下的声音，俗话称“听冰声”。听冰声，指渔把头把耳朵贴在冰面上，他通过水流声，能分辨出鱼群的位置。

As the saying goes, the fishing master must know his ice, meaning that he knows how to read the color of the ice. In winter, fish tend to gather in groups under ice. As the fish gather, the water surges, causing the snow on the ice to swell slightly. An ice surface like this is a sign of fish beneath. Next, the master looks at the colors. The area of ice with fish underneath tends to have several bubbles in it, and the bubbles are clustered where the fish are swimming, in which case the ice would be gray. The master also knows how to listen for sounds below the ice, called "hearing the ice." He does so by pressing an ear on the ice and listening to the sounds of the flowing water, by which he is able to locate the position of the fish.

冬天捕鱼，几乎就是比渔把头们谁能分辨鱼群居住位置的本领。上冰打鱼是集体行动，就是要"快"，人拖泥带水不行。但这种快的成功与否，又全靠把头的能力。

Winter fishing depends almost solely on the fishing master's ability to determine where the fish are. Fishing on the ice is a collective effort, and the emphasis is on speed; dillydallying will never do. However, whether this speed will result in success falls entirely on the shoulders of the fishing master and his skills.

全网的伙计到了冰上，把头要迅速识别在哪凿冰下网。全伙人都准备好，甚至运好了气，单等把头一声令下。把头识冰，全靠经验。有时别看这儿有一伙人正在凿冰，但把头一看，他们那凿法已把鱼赶跑了。跑向哪？如果是东北风，冰的西北口处保准有鱼被震撵到那儿去了。

来在冰上展宏图
A Grand Hunt

归理冰网
Cleaning the Icy Net

With all the fishing crew on the ice, the fishing master must quickly determine where to make the ice holes and cast the net. The whole group is ready now, some have even taken a deep breath in preparation, just waiting for the order from the fishing master. And it all comes down to his experience in reading the ice. Sometimes there will be a group of fishermen chiseling ice, but the fishing master takes one look and knows that the way there are chiseling has scared the fish away. Where did the fish go? If a northeaster happens to be blowing, then some of the fish driven away by the chiseling must be in the northwest corner.

到了把头约莫估计鱼群走的地窝子，立刻手一挥说："插旗！"这时，打眼的二话不说，跟着抱旗的跑到把头告诉的地方，立刻把旗插在冰上，开始凿冰打眼，不许再问话，就是快干。那边冰镩子砸冰声一响，这边解马，卸网，固定马轮子，一切的一切要立刻开始，不允许丝毫的怠慢。这种"抢窝子"，有时也是指渔把头来得"早"不如来得"巧"。

When he has a good idea of where the fish are, he gives a decisive wave of his hand and says, "Flag!" The crew in charge of chiseling ice eyes immediately follows the flag carrier to the site indicated by the master, where the flag is erected and the chiseling begins; no questions asked, fast work is the key. As soon as the sound of the chisel hitting the ice can be heard, other crew members unhitch the horses, unload the nets and secure the horse winch. Everything must kick off immediately, and no dithering is allowed. In the race to find the right spot for casting the net, sometimes it is more about the fishing master being there at the right time than being there early.

老渔把头说，在查干淖尔，我闭着眼也能知道东南西北。我坐在冰上，用鼻子一嗅，就知道哪儿是北大堵方向，哪儿是河神庙，哪儿是白道口，哪是大口门，哪儿是青山头。这儿的雪、冰和地气，都和我处熟了。

The old fishing master says: In Chagan Nur, I can tell the directions even with my eyes shut. When I sit on the ice, I take a sniff and I know in which direction Beidadu is located, where the River God Temper is, where Baidaokou is, where Damenkou is, where Qingshantou is...The snow, the ice and the air here...we are old friends.

隆冬时节，古老的查干淖尔冰面闪着灰色的光泽，那是天空的乌云把白雪涂成了灰色，如果太阳不出来，一冬天都是这样。老北风一起，茫茫的冰面上灰蒙蒙一片，什么也看不清，怎么能分辨出鱼在冰下的位置呢?

In deep winter, the ancient Chagan Nur ice sheet glitters with shades of gray, for the dark clouds in the sky have painted the snow this color. If the sun does not come out, it is like this all through winter. When the north wind blows, the ice is shrouded in a flurry of gray and everything becomes a blur. How then can one tell where the fish are underneath the ice?

但是，查干淖尔的渔民有办法。这儿的古语说：人知鱼性，这话一点也不假。鱼儿生活在水中，它们其实最识水性，人要知鱼性，必须先知水性。在查干淖尔这样大的水域之中，老渔把头找鱼，先要掌握水。首先，他要牢牢记住夏秋季节泡子里哪个方位涨水，哪儿涝了。涨水、涝水鱼儿都有变化。水一大，鱼走尽了；而水深处，常常是鱼越冬喜欢居住之地。在夏秋时渔把头就要记住这一切。第二就是仔细分析泡子封冻的时间。查干淖尔“封泡”（水结冰称为封泡），每年时间并不一样。封泡早与晚，完全与风有关。如果是东北风封的泡，冬捕时就往偏南的泡地选窝子，因东北风往往把鱼“赶”到了南边一带；如果是西北风封的泡，则要选东南方一带挑选鱼窝子。当然，还要看封泡那一夜刮没刮雪，雪片落泡，影响鱼的一冬天选位。所以冰面上某处积雪的深浅、薄厚、大小，都与鱼的多少有直接关系。第三要看坡。坡，指坡度。查干淖尔的湖底往往和平原土地一样，也有高矮坡地之分，而鱼喜欢在坡下一带居住。冬天，鱼的活动能力低，相比夏秋，它不太爱游走。因此它们往往喜欢找水深的地方，那儿的温度高些，坡地挡水守水，所以是它们居住的理想之处。

The Chagan Nur fishermen have a way. An old saying here goes: People know how fish behave. These words hold truth. Fish live in water, so they know water the best. To know how the fish behave, people must first understand how water behaves. So too the fishing master must know the water before he can find the fish in such a large body of water as Chagan Nur. First, he must pay attention to and remember what happened in the lake in summer and autumn: Where did the water swell, and where did it flood, etc., because it all has an impact on the fish. When there is too much water, the fish are gone; often, deep water is where the fish like to cluster in winter. The fishing master must remember all this from summer and autumn. Second, he must do a careful analysis of the time at which the lake froze over. The Chagan Nur is "sealed" (meaning freezing over) at a different time each year, and it is completely related to the wind. If a northeaster seals the lake, then the net casting sites for winter fishing should be chosen from the southern part of the lake, since the northeaster often drives the fish to the south; when a northwester seals the lake, then the net casing sites should be picked towards the southeast. Of course, it also depends on whether it snowed on the night that the lake froze over. Snowfall into the lake will affect where the fish stays all winter. The depth and distribution of snow over a certain area of the lake surface is directly related to the number of fish underneath the ice. Third, the fishing master looks at the slope. Just like plains on dry land, the terrain at the bottom of the Chagan Nur undulates with steep slopes and low slopes. Fish prefer to live at the bottom of slope areas. Compared to summer

and autumn, in winter, the fish are less active and do not move around much. So they often stay in deeper water where the temperature is higher and the slopes help retain water. Those are ideal winter dwellings for them.

摄影 / 刘玉忱
Photograph by / Liu Yuchen

把头还要会看“鱼花”。鱼花，又叫鱼泡泡，是鱼喘息时吐出的气。在冬天，鱼喘出的气会在冰中形成一层一层的泡，这叫鱼花，说明这儿冰底下有鱼。而鱼花又分“新花”和“旧花”，又叫“老花”。新花，是鱼刚吐的，或昨晚上吐的，特征是这些“花”在冰水里还在晃动、晃荡，说明有鱼群，把头正好可以指挥人在此凿冰下网。而旧花，是指那些已冻结在冰层里的泡泡。这些“花”一动也不动，说明鱼群已经过去了。不懂鱼性的人才会在旧花处凿冰开眼。

The fishing master must also be able to read “fish flower”, also known as fish bubble, which is gas exhaled by fish that escapes as bubbles. In winter, the gas forms layers and layers of bubbles in the ice, i.e., fish flower, indicating the presence of fish underneath. Fish flowers are divided into “new flowers” and “old flowers”. The new flowers are fresh bubbles just made by the fish or the night before, and are still quivering and floating in the icy water, which indicates that the fish are still there. This is where the fishing master will have his team chisel the ice and cast the net. The old flowers are bubbles that are already frozen in the ice. These “flowers” do not move, indicating that the fish have already left. Only people who don’t understand fish behavior will make ice holes where the “old flowers” are.

“花”还分多种，有一种花称为“草花”，把头会一眼认出。草花，是水里的草吐出的气泡。冬天草一冻也会吐气泡，称为草花。草花的特征是一冒到顶，形状是一串一串的，被渔民称为“串泡”。鱼花则是一层一层，一片一片的，有明显的区别。这些本事都是老渔把头的看家本领。

The “flower” can be further divided into different categories. There is the “grass flower”, which the fishing master can recognize instantly. They are bubbles made by water grass, and their most distinctive feature is that the bubbles rise to the top in strings, and are called “string bubbles” by the fishermen. The fish flowers are recognizably different from grass flowers in that they form in layers and patches. Knowing all this is what makes the fishing master a fishing master.

在查干淖尔，冬季捕鱼网上冰前，要先选出领网的，领网的人往往被冬捕的人称为二把头。顾名思义，领网，就是指带领这伙人实际在冰上作业。当把头观察完下网点，他还有诸多的事情要做，什么卖鱼呀，接待来客呀，都由把头去做，于是冰上的活就交给领网把头领着去干。领网把头要懂得捕鱼各个环节中的规俗和技术，比如需要“穿草鞋”或“摘挂子”时，领网的要及时发现，并组织和指派“跟网的”去处理。领网人，心眼要正，一碗水要端平；该谁的活，就由谁去干，不能看人下菜碟。不然时间长了，他在冰面上没有威信，跟网的就会和他有二心。

Before winter fishing begins in Chagan Nur, the fishermen also have to elect the net leader, who is known as the number two man after the fishing master. As the name suggests, the net leader refers to the person who leads the fishing crew in actual operations on the ice. After deciding on the net casting spots, the fishing master has many other tasks to attend to, such as selling the fish, receiving guests, etc., so command is handed over to the net leader. The net

严寒凝固的查干淖尔
Chagan Nur Frozen by the Cold

leader must have mastered the customs and techniques relating to various aspects of winter fishing. For instance, if the need arises to "put on grass shoes" or "disentangle the net", the net leader must promptly identify the problem and assign the "net handlers" to deal with it. The net leader must be impartial in allocating work, assigning tasks to whoever should be responsible, showing no favoritism. Otherwise, over time he will lose his authority on the ice and the loyalty of the net handlers.

冬捕中"穿草鞋"，其实不是真草鞋，而是用谷草或稻草拧成的草把。冬季冰下捕鱼，是技术性很强的一种渔猎活动，要把偌大的网在冰层下展开，而送网要从事先凿开的冰眼（冰洞）下网，由于冰下的泥地都不是一码平地，有时就是草根、树茬、稀泥、高岗或大坑，不利于网的送运，就得"穿草鞋"。穿草鞋又叫"拴草鞋"，是指在网进入到这样的地段时，在网边底绑上一个个草把，使网在冰层底下的塘泥上便于滑动。于是这穿草鞋就成了捕鱼过程中的一道绝活。

In winter fishing, "putting on grass shoes" is not used in the literal sense. The grass shoe in fact refers to a bundle of straw. Winter ice fishing is highly technical, where a large net is spread under ice through ice holes chiseled in advance, and the terrain beneath the ice is not always flat and smooth. In some places the surface is covered with grassroots, tree stubbles, mud, hillocks or big pits that hinder the net's movement. Such occasions call for "putting on grass shoes". Also called "tying on grass shoes", it means tying straw bundles under the net when it enters rough terrain to make it easier for the net to slide along the mud beneath the ice. This is another highly technical task in the process of winter fishing.

在网由冰眼下到冰底时，把头在冰面上来回走动，观察网运送的速度，一旦发现网走得慢了，就知有不顺畅的地方了，于是就大喊："穿草鞋！"

摄影 / 刘玉忱
Photograph by / Liu Yuchen

把头的话，就等于命令一样。这时，专门有一个叫“打串连”的人，答应一声，立刻抄起“串连杆子”（一种六米至九米长的杆子，头上有一个尖，顶上带个钩）把一捆谷草勾在上面，然后从出问题最近的网眼下杆子，将杆子和谷草捆对准那儿的网扣，手腕一打，杆子带着谷草捆顺直往前运行，并准确地垫在网下的不平处。这就叫“穿草鞋”或“拴草鞋”。查干淖尔冬捕渔队中有诸多的打串连“穿草鞋”的能手。这些人一要迅速理解渔把头的意图；二要及时判断网在冰层下的复杂情况；三要会用腕劲。

When the net is cast from the ice eye to spread under the ice, the fishing master walks back and forth on the ice to observe the progress. If there is a delay, he knows that the net has run into a rough spot, at which point he will call out: “Put on the grass shoes!”

long, with a pointed end attached to a hook) answers in response and immediately grabs hold of the pole. He hooks a bundle of straws onto the pole, lowers the pole into the ice hole closest to the trouble spot, aims the pole and the straw bundle at the net buckle, and shakes his wrists. The pole, along with the straw bundle, travels forward and the bundle lands right where the uneven spot is under the net. This is what "putting on grass shoes" means. There are a number of skilled hook pole handlers who can perform this task in the Chagan Nur winter fishing teams. They must first be able to quickly understand the intention of the fishing master; second, promptly assess the situation of the net under the ice; and third, know how to use their wrist strength.

1 拨动岁月的网纲（左1）

2 堆砌岁月的网山（中2）

3 梳理岁月的网片（右3）

1-3: Working the Nets

了挂草鞋的地方，杆勾一定会与草捆自动脱离，不然不但送不好草鞋，还会影响网的整体运行，这就全靠手劲了。

This "wrist strength", or "wrist skill" is extremely important. When the pole handler sends the pole in from the ice hole, the pole with the straw bundle attached to it must travel smoothly under the ice, and once they reach the uneven spot where the bundle must land, the pole hook must automatically separate from the bundle; otherwise not only is the grass shoe task bungled, but the overall operation of the net is also affected. The key to avoiding this lies in the wrist strength.

为了练打串连杆子的本领，查干淖尔人平时就玩"串老头"和"打瓦"，这都是嫩科尔沁草原和湖泊一带牧民和农民人人喜爱玩的一种民间游戏。其实这不是在"玩"，是在坚持传承古老的渔猎技艺，渔夫们往往从很小就接触到了这种活动。"串老头"是用树条或高粱秆做用具，比谁能在五米或十米开外的土地坷垃或石头，通过抛、撇来击中目标，以决输赢……这一切活动，从小就练就了查干淖尔渔夫们捕鱼时使串连杆子"拴草鞋"的本领。

To practice using the hook pole, fishermen at Chagan Nur often play two games, called "string of old men" and "hitting tiles". These are folk games popular among herdsmen and farmers on the Nen-Horqin Grassland and in the lake area. In fact, this is not "play", but a way of preserving the ancient legacy of fishing skills that fishermen are exposed to at a young age. "String of old men" involves using tree twigs or sorghum stalks to shoot at mud bricks that are five or ten meters away. The one who misses the target is the loser and the one who hits the target is the winner. "Hitting tiles" is a similar game, but is often played using rubbles or stones to hit the target. Such activities, engaged in since childhood, help the fishermen of Chagan Nur develop the skills needed to maneuver the hook pole and "put on the grass shoes".

渔夫与网的舞蹈——自然的恋歌
Of Fishermen and Nets

查干淖尔冬季捕捞出的鱼味道是那么的鲜美，可是鱼儿却是打鱼人用命换来的，其中摘挂子就是一种玩命的“绝活”。往冰层下送网，并不是很顺利，如果单单是冰层底下不平不滑，“穿草鞋”也就解决了，可问题是有时不是穿“草鞋”就能够解决的，那就是网在冰层底被树根茬或石头死死地刮住，必须要有人下去处理才行，这就是渔民俗语说的“摘挂子”。

The winter fish from Chagan Nur are fresh and delicious, but they are caught by fishermen who risk their lives. One of the life-threatening feats is “untangling the net”. Spreading the net under ice does not always go smoothly. If the problem is simply a bumpy area at the lake bottom, “putting on grass shoes” will solve it. However, sometimes resolving the problem requires more than that. For instance, in the case that the net is caught by a tree stubble or a stone, someone must go beneath the ice and into the water to deal with it. This is what the fishermen call “untangling the net”.

摘挂子的人不但要水性好，而且还要会在冰层下换气，同时动作要迅速。这是把头教给徒弟的“绝活”，因为户外的气温已下降到零下四十度了，冰层下的水温也在零下呀。时间一长，人的心脏功能减弱，血管温度降低，人就会窒息而亡。而人一旦出水，上面的人要立刻抢救。先是把人用棉被一裹，立刻扛到网房子里去，但一定不能马上烤火。因这时人的肌肉和皮肤已经冻结，烤火加热就会脱落，血管和肌肉坏死就不可救了。有足够冬捕经验的查干淖尔人一见摘挂子的人上了冰面，要立刻将此人用棉被卷上，扛到网房子外屋，展开棉被，先用白雪给冻昏迷的人搓身子。白雪这时就成了救人的药。

The person in charge of the untangling must not only be a good swimmer, but also know how to breathe under ice. He must be quick as well. It is one of the skills that is taught by a master to his apprentice. With the outdoor temperature below minus forty degrees, and the water temperature below zero, being in the water for too long can lead to weakened heart function and lowered blood vessel temperature, which can cause death by suffocation. Once the person is out of the water, the people on the ice must immediately come to his aid. First, the person is wrapped up in a quilt and immediately carried to the net shed. But he must not be warmed by the fire yet, because his muscles and skin are frozen, and heating by fire will cause them to peel off, leading to necrosis of the blood vessels and muscles, by which point there will be no bringing him back. As soon as the person who untangles the net returns to the ice surface, the experienced winter fisherman will immediately wrap him in a quilt, carry him to the outer room of the net shed, unfurl the quilt, and rub snow on the person who has passed out from the cold. The white snow then becomes a life-saving medicine.

1 冰与网的依恋（上1）

2 网山的背景与空间（下2）

1-2 Of Ice and Net

搓时，要先搓胸口和手脚及耳朵。因胸口不搓热，心脏就会在短时间内丧失功能，不能调动周身的细胞使人复活；而手脚和耳朵，都是人体的神经末梢，动作稍慢点儿，这些部位马上就变黑，血液凝固，从此烂掉。经过一阵冻雪猛搓，人才会有了知觉。这时，还不能马上抬上炕去，还要接着帮他活动手脚，并给他灌上微微一小盅烧酒。当他脸上有了点血色，才立刻抬到火炕上去。所谓领网的处事要正，这在今天集体渔业捕捞过程中有许多方面体现得已经不太明显，而在从前，各“小股子”（跟网的）统统都是自己带着捕鱼工具前来入股，下网时怎么使，怎么用，完全由领网把头说了算。特别是网从冰眼里拖出来时要迅速洗净，然后上垛、码好。不然时间一长，网容易冻，坏得快，这就费网。所以领网的把头指挥哪片网先叠快码，谁先干哪块活，都是很有说道的。冬网的集体劳作使分工越来越细，这使得一伙冬网谁也离不开谁，大家相互制约，又互相发挥着作用，于是促成一种文化和规俗按着地域和捕鱼行业的道德观念完善和传承着。

The chest, hands, feet and ears should be rubbed first. If the chest is not rubbed warm, the heart will quickly lose its function; the hands, feet and ears all contain nerve endings, and the slightest delay in warming them will cause them to quickly turn black and putrefy due to blood coagulation. After a robust rubbing with snow, the person will gradually regain consciousness, but still he must not be carried to the *kang* (bed-stove). Someone must first help him move his hands and feet a bit and give him some liquor. When his face regains some color, then it is time to put him on the *kang*.

Although it is said that the net leader must be impartial, in many respects, this is not so clearly reflected in today's collective fishing. In the past, the "small shares" (net handlers) brought their own fishing tools when they joined the fishing crew and became shareholders; how they used their nets was entirely dictated by the net leader. When a net is pulled out from the ice hole, it needs to be cleaned quickly, piled and stacked; otherwise, the net is often frozen and could easily break, which means it would have to be replaced more often. Therefore, much can be made of the net leader's orders as to which net should be folded and stacked first, or which net should be used where. The collective nature of winter fishing has led to more and more division of labor, which means in a winter fishing group everyone depends on one another, restricting one another while each making their own contribution. This has given rise to a culture and conventions that follow the mores of a specific region and trade, while improving on them and preserving them.

冰车、冰爬和冰绞轮
Cart, Sledge and Winch on the Ice

跟网，就是指直接操网的捕鱼人。这是一个冬捕网队的主要劳力，其中又有许多详细的分工。冬季，冰面上奇寒无比，出冰的网如不迅速倒向一方，往往会打卷拖坏，这活要麻利。同时，拖网的还要摘鱼，就是把挂在网上的小鱼小虾什么的，一个一个捡净。这一是使网保持干净清洁，同时也是防止网上的鱼虾在夜间招引野狼野狗前来撕网，保护网的安全。更重要的是传承着一种古老的查干淖尔人的生存品质。

把心爱的娘子拥在怀中
Holding the tool of my trade in my arms.

Net handlers are the fishermen who directly handle the net. They are the main labor force on a winter fishing net team. There is much division of labor in this area as well. In the extreme cold on the ice, when the net is brought out from the water and onto the ice, if the net is not quickly tilted to one side, it is likely to curl and be damaged while it is dragged over the ice; so it is work that must be carried out efficiently. Meanwhile, those dragging the net are also responsible for picking the small fish and shrimps from the net. This keeps the net clean and protects the net from being torn by wolves or wild dogs that come in the night, having been attracted by the fish and shrimps that were left on the net. More importantly, it is about upholding a respect for the net that the Chagan Nur people have had since ancient times.

敬网，就是要恭恭敬敬地对待网、保护好网，网用了一冬天，也累了一冬天！它帮助渔民挣到了钱，又改善了生活，查干淖尔人要尊敬它、感谢它、恭敬它。同时“敬”又是“净”，是将网冲洗干净，在有沙地的高岗上冲洗，并摘掉网上的小鱼小虾，以免遭老鼠或其他动物啃咬，损坏网；草也摘净，以免昆虫或动物啃咬，摘掉草鞋，进行修补、封存，待下一年冬季再发挥它的作用。这是珍贵的渔猎文化。

Respecting the net means treating the net with respect and protecting it. It too has worked all winter and must be exhausted. It helps the fishermen make a living and improve their lives, and the people of Chagan Nur must show respect, gratitude and reverence for the net. In Chinese, the character for “respect” is homophonous with the character for “clean”, so respecting the net means also to keep it clean. The washing is done on a sandy hill, during which time small fish and shrimps are removed from the net to prevent rats and other creatures from gnawing and damaging it. Grass is also removed to prevent insects or animals from nesting in the net. The “grass shoes” are taken off. The net is repaired and put away until next winter, when it will again play its role. This is also part of the precious fishing culture at Chagan Nur.

跟网的还要时时修网。网在冰下作业，往往会被石砂、泥块、树根、草茬子刮坏。有时会被鱼嘴鱼鳞划断，有的鱼也咬网扎网。这样，时时补网就成了跟网人的活计。跟网的人每人兜里都揣着线绳和补网的工具，一旦发现出冰的网破损，要立刻修补。

The net operators are constantly repairing their nets. Used under the ice, the net is often scraped and damaged by stones, sand, mud blocks, tree roots and grassroots. Sometimes fish mouths or fish scales can severed the net, and there are fish that bite or otherwise damage the net. Thus it is the net operator’s never-ending job to repair the net. Every net operator carries ropes and other tools so they can immediately make repairs if the net comes out of the water damaged.

拖拉时的心曲
Hauling in the Net.

这些活计都要由跟网的小股子干。小股子是冬捕网上最普通劳力的称呼，就像学徒工或是“小打”一样的。“股”，指一个劳力，一个“股份”之意。因从前打鱼都是一伙人互相凑在一起来进行，这就有各自带来的工具不同，人的名望的不同，年龄的不同，能力的不同等等，所以把整体利益所得分割成若干“股”，于是一个基本劳力就算一个“股”，分解到一个人就被称为“一股子”，所以一个基本劳力就叫小股子了。小股子在冰上作业也有分工，主要是网队上的力气活和杂活，不带多少技术性，都由小股子去完成。比如说冬捕冰上最多的活计是“拉套网”，就都由小股子去干。

All this work is done by the "small shares" who operate the nets. "Small share" is how the most common laborer on the winter net team is referred to, like an apprentice or a novice. A "share" means a worker with one share of the labor. In the past, fishing was carried out by a group of people who randomly came together. They brought different tools to the collective effort, and were different in terms of reputation, age, skill level, etc. The profit was divided into several shares, with one basic unit of labor receiving one share. And so a basic laborer became known as a "small share" fisherman. There is division of labor among the small shares working on the ice as well. Most of the net team's manual work and chores, which require little technical skills, are done by small shares. For example, most of the winter fishing work on the ice involves "pulling the nets", which would fall on the small shares to do.

拉套网，又叫“拉套的”，是指当网从冰眼里出来时，大绦的一头由马轮子拖，而网边和网身要时时有人去拖拉和保护，这就由拉套小股子去做，俗称拉网小股子。还有什么“跟马小股子”“镩冰小股子”“抄鱼小股子”等等，总之，网上方方面面的力气活，都由他们去干。小股子是一个渔把头的童年。就是说，每个渔把头都是由小股子一点一点“熬”过来的。开始当小股子，然后当跟网的，领网的，最后才能当上把头；如果连小股子的活计都干不了，那这个人是一辈子也当不上渔把头的，这就叫“多年的媳妇熬成婆”。

壮丽的渔猎阵脚
Magnificent Fishing Array

When the net comes out of the ice eye, while one end of the big braid rope is pulled by the horse-drawn winch, there needs to be people who stay at the side of the net to help haul and protect it—this is what "pulling the nets", or "pulling the set", refers to, and which is performed

by the "net-pulling small shares". There are also "horse-tending small shares", "ice-chiseling small shares", "fish-ladling small shares", etc. In short, all the manual work related to the net is carried out by them. A small share is a fishing master in his childhood. That is to say, every fishing master made it to where they are now by being a small share first. They started out as small shares, then became net leaders, and finally they were masters. If a man cannot do the work of a small share, he will never become a fishing master. It rather fits the Chinese saying: The long-suffering daughter-in-law will become a mother-in-law one day.

查干淖尔冬捕，把头和他当小股子的故事一辈子也说不完。打鱼打鱼，网房子就是一个世界；啥人都有，啥事都能遇上啊。“马拉子”，就是冬季捕鱼赶马轮的人，又叫“喂马的”，这也是一伙网队里非常重要的角色。北方平原把马儿养得浑圆而健壮，马对这里的人有一种与生俱来的依赖，马和与它生活在一起的人是很熟悉的。这是因为像马拉子这样的一些人都了解马。在北方，了解马，就是了解人自己。首先马拉子要会“挑马”、“相马”，所以人们往往又管马拉子叫马把式。

The fishing master has endless stories to tell about winter fishing in Chagan Nur and his past as a small share fisherman. In the realm of fishing, the net shed is a world unto itself; you encounter everyone and everything there is to encounter. In the net team there is another important figure, that of the "horse-puller", or "horse feeder", who is in charge of the horse winch operations. Nurtured by the northern plains, the horses here are sturdy and strong. They seem to have an innate dependence on the people here, especially those who are a familiar presence in their lives, such as the horse-pullers, who truly understand horses. In the north, to understand horses is to understand people. The horse-puller must first and foremost be able to pick horses and assess horses, that is why they are often called horse masters as well.

马拉子不但会选马，还要会“使马”。冬天马在冰上拉马轮子奔走，十分不易，首先马拉子要心疼马儿。赶马轮子的人讲究会使鞭，他绝不用鞭子抽打马，特别是不能用鞭子伤了马的耳朵和眼睛。他往往通过吆喝和挥手、踹脚、用胳膊去碰等声音和动作，来给马以快、慢、紧、缓的拉动信号；他一般不使鞭子抽马，他往往在马头和马耳朵的上方甩动响鞭，以此驱动马奔走。

The horse-puller does more than pick horses; he also has to know how to use them. To go round and round on ice pulling the winch is grueling work, and the horse-puller must know this and treat the horses with kindness. While driving the horses to pull the wheel, he is careful about how he uses his whip. He will never whip the horse, especially not around the horse's ears and eyes. He gives the horses orders to move faster or slower through sounds and gestures, by calling out, waving his hands, stamping his feet, touching the horse with his arm, etc. He generally does not whip the horse; instead, he will crack the whip over the horse's head or ears to urge the horse on.

冬季冰上赶马，不同于马在路上拉车或犁地，这是使马转圈儿走，而马拉子又和马紧紧靠在一起，所以他非常熟悉各匹马的力气和脾气，并且他要时时地注意，自己别被马踩着，要学会“躲”。再就是马拉子一定要会喂马。

Driving horses to walk in circles on winter ice is different from making them pull carts or plough fields. The horse-puller stays close to the horses, so he is familiar with each horse's strength and temperament. Meanwhile, he needs to be careful not to be trampled by the horses, so he must learn to "dodge". Another thing that the horse-puller must know is how to feed the horses.

马拉子又叫“喂马的”是有道理的。这些马拖着上千斤的分量整日在冰上奔跑，体力消耗很大。套子马讲究吃好喂好，夜间马拉子一定要起来泡一盆豆饼水让马喝了，以便增加马抵抗严寒的能力。对于那种不懂马不疼马的马拉子，冬捕的渔把头坚决不要。同时，马拉子还要会挂马掌。

There is a reason why the horse-puller is also called the "horse feeder". Running all day on the ice while pulling weights of some five hundred kilograms requires a lot of physical exertion, and keeping the horses well-fed is essential. The horse feeder must get up at night to soak a pot of soybean cake water, which he gives to the horses to increase their resistance against the cold. Those horse-pullers who don't understand or care about the horses will be firmly rejected by the fishing master during winter fishing. Another thing that the horse-puller must know is how to attach horseshoes.

挂马掌在查干淖尔是指给在冰上拉马轮子的马挂掌的一种绝活手艺。查干淖尔的渔夫们个个都是使马养马选马的能手，他们深知马的习性，也特别知道疼马。在冬季的查干淖尔，马和别处的不一样。这儿的马，冬季在冰上拉网奔走，它们的脚上挂着的掌不是皮掌或铁盘掌，而是一种叫“串钉子”的掌。

脸上的冰霜才是渔夫的家当
A fisherman's wealth is the ice and frost on his face.

一脸冰霜，全部家当
A Frost-Covered Face, A Fisherman's Fate

In Chagan Nur, attaching horseshoes refers to putting on horseshoes for the horses that pull the winches on the ice. All the fishermen here are experts in using, grooming and picking horses. They know all the horses' habits and especially how to treat them well. The horses of Chagan Nur in winter are different from horses in other regions. Here, the horses pull the net while running on ice. The horseshoes that they wear are not leather or iron, but something called "string nails".

在这儿，铁匠炉的铁匠们不用问，只要是冬季牵马来的人，他们准知道是上冰。给上冰的马挂掌，就决定了铁匠的手法。串钉子掌叫"挂"，挂是马蹄子的铁盘，先打上铁盘，到冰上一走一磨，串钉立刻出现，咬在冰上"嘎嘎咔咔"地响，就成了串钉（或叫"攒丁"）。

Here, the blacksmiths know that when someone brings their horses to them in winter, it is to prepare them for the ice, and this determines how the blacksmith makes the horseshoe. Fitting horses here with the string nail horseshoe is called "hanging". The iron plate is fixed first. When the horse walks on ice and grinds the plate, the string nails immediately appear, biting the ice and making a crushing sound. Now the horseshoe has become the string nails horseshoe (or called "saving nail").

这种绝活绝艺，只有查干淖尔的铁匠们会，而大多数渔把头也会，不然就得花钱去打。为了生存，渔把头们什么活计都学在手。这种绝活的技艺在"掌叶子"上。掌叶子是钉在马蹄子上的"盘"，叶子半壳里打上掌钉。当拉马轮子的马在冰上一使劲儿，那串钉立刻出来咬住了冰，使马在冰上不打滑，蹄能咬住亮冰地，用上劲地拉网拖绦。等一趟网下来，要立刻给马换掌叶子，这一换，直接把串钉带下来了。但如果手艺不好的铁匠或渔把头，把串钉镶得过深或过浅，不等马走到网眼就露钉子，这就不是好手艺。掌叶子的串钉为三角形，带膀带翅。给拉马轮子的马换串钉掌，都得老铁匠或老渔把头亲自去干。

Only the blacksmiths in Chagan Nur have mastered the unique skill of making this kind of horseshoe, as have most of the fishing masters; otherwise they would have to pay someone else to do it. In order to survive, the fishing masters learn to master all kinds of skills. The secret to making string nails horseshoes lies in the "hoof leaf". The hoof leaf is the "plate" that is nailed to the horse hoof. Half of the leaf is studded. When the winch horses exert force on the ice, the string nails are exposed and bite the

背负着自然的理念
An Entire Culture on His Back

ice so that the horses will not slip on the ice; their hooves then have traction on the ice and they are able to exert real force while pulling in the big braid rope. When one net has been dragged out, the plate leaf must be immediately removed, which also removes the string nails. However, a less skilled blacksmith or fishing master may set the string nails too deep or too shallow, resulting in the nails popping out before the horses even reach the net eye. That is an example of poor craftsmanship. The string studs of the plate leaf are triangular with wings. Fitting the horses with new string nail plates is something that only veteran blacksmiths or fishing masters can do.

冬捕，从凿冰下网到起网，往往需要漫长的过程，于是夜里冰面上就要留人看守网棚。寒冷的冬季，茫茫的冰面，空荡且荒凉。凿开的冰层已透了气。鱼的气味已浓浓地升起来，弥漫在大地的空气里，连冰块和雪花中都饱含着鱼的鲜嫩气味儿，于是鱼鲜气息招来许许多多的"不速之客"。本来冰面已经没有了鱼，因为当天网上的鱼当天就拉回渔场去了。可是，一些小的鱼，或摔掉的鱼肉碎片，以及没有运走的网上挂着的小鱼虾，这些都成了冬夜四处觅食的动物们的目标。

From making ice holes, casting the net to extracting the net, winter fishing can take a long time, so someone must stay on the ice at night to keep guard at the net shed. The vast expanse of ice in the cold winter is empty and desolate. The chiseled ice has exposed the water, and the thick smell of fish has risen and filled the air. Even the ice blocks and snowflakes are imbued with the smell of fresh fish, which attracts many uninvited guests. There are no more fish on the ice, for the catch that day has already been transported back to the fishery, but there are some small fish and morsels that broke off from the big fish on the ice, and some small fish and shrimps hanging on the net. These become targets for animals foraging in the winter night.

觅食本来是世间一切生灵的合理行为，可是查干淖尔冬夜里的这些不速之客往往在寻找吃食的同时，不是撕碎了网片，就是扒破了出网的地方，使第二天的捕鱼无法进行。每年一到了大雪纷飞的季节，北方的冰野气温下降到零下40多度，冰天雪地里，许多动物又冻又饿，觅食就成了动物们最后的挣扎……

Foraging is what all living creatures rightfully do, but the uninvited guests in the winter nights of Chagan Nur often tear up the nets or damage the net extraction site in their search for food, hampering the fishing activity the following day. Each year, when the blizzard blows, when the temperature drops to minus 40 degrees on the icy northern wilderness, many animals, cold and hungry, resort to scavenging as they struggle to survive...

古诗里形容，寒冬，“千山鸟飞绝，万径人踪灭。”一切生灵为了争口“食”而外出奔波，于是每当大雪纷飞的严冬，在那些奇寒无比的冬捕的日子里，渔民们每夜都准备些小鱼，主动地喂给那些在冬季里冻得、饿得已筋疲力尽的觅食的动物们吃，吃饱了它们也便走了。

In winter, to quote a poem from the Tang dynasty, “all the birds in a thousand mountains have flown away, and all traces of humans have disappeared from ten thousand paths.” In this desolate season, when creatures venture out looking for food in the bitter cold night, the fishermen of Chagan Nur always have some small fish ready, which they give to the freezing, hungry and helpless animals. Once fed, the animals leave.

他们还在捕鱼下网的窝子上立一个牌，上面清清楚楚地标着：小心，保护那些饥饿的觅食动物。这些招牌在查干淖尔的冰面上随处可见。

The fishermen even put up a sign at the fishing site, which reads: “Attention, protect the hungry foraging animals.” These signs can be seen everywhere on the ice in Chagan Nur.

当科尔沁的狂风暴雪日夜吹刮的时候，当风停雪住，月亮出来照耀着茫茫雪野的时候，人们就会亲眼看见许许多多的生命在主动地靠近着查干淖尔渔人的窝棚，它们是狐狸、狼，甚至还有兔子……有了好心的查干淖尔渔夫为它们准备的吃喝，它们再也不去扒动渔人的网和出网口了，渔夫们再也不用操心动物来骚扰啦！

让遗产固定在冰原上
Fixing the nets and keeping an icy legacy alive.

The blizzard often blows day and night in Horqin. However, when the wind and snow subside, and the moon shines down on the snowy wilderness, you will see a great many creatures approaching the fishermen’s shack in Chagan Nur: Foxes, wolves, even hares... With the food that the kind-hearted fishermen have prepared for them, they no longer forage in the nets or the net holes, and the fishermen no longer worry about being harassed by hungry animals!

其实大自然是一个合理的存在，它在默默地平衡着人世间的一切事物的发展，它本身就存在着一个正确的运行规律，只是有的时候，人们并没有细心地去寻找到它。而寻找到这种人与自然与共的本质规律，需要人的精神和思想的付出。查干淖尔人，是在自觉地把自己融入生活和自然的历程中的人，所以他们得到了自然的真诚的回报，也使自己成为大自然的最亲密的朋友和伙伴。

In fact, nature is most judicious. Quietly, it balances the development of all things on earth. There is a rule by which everything should operate, it is just that people sometimes fail to pay attention and try to find it. Finding this inherent rule governing the coexistence of man and nature requires people to devote their spirit and thought. The people of Chagan Nur consciously try to make themselves part of the course of life and nature, and have in turn received the good will of nature. As such, they have become nature's most intimate friend and partner.

查干淖尔，处处充满了传承。人的一言一行，一举一动，都受到一种严格的心理制约。他们懂得如何打鱼，因为这里传承和弥漫着一种优秀的文化氛围。

Chagan Nur is a place filled with traditions. These traditions have conditioned the people's every word, every deed and every move. They know how to fish because of the cultural environment that they have inherited and is all pervasive here.

遗产的步骤

Legacy in Action

北方渔猎——忙碌的冰原
Northern fishing—the ice field bustles with activity.

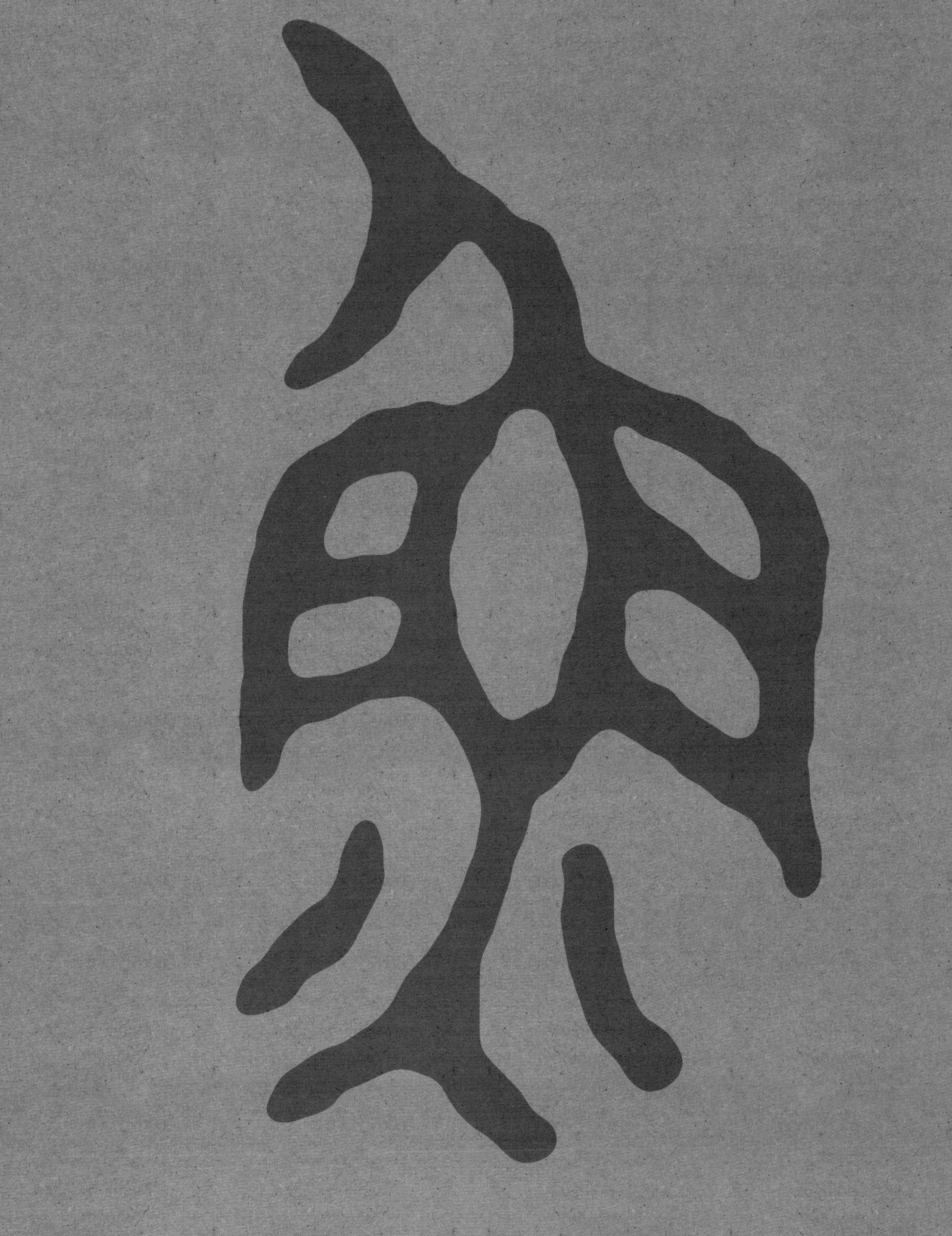

A Flourishing Fishing Culture

鱼舞盛世

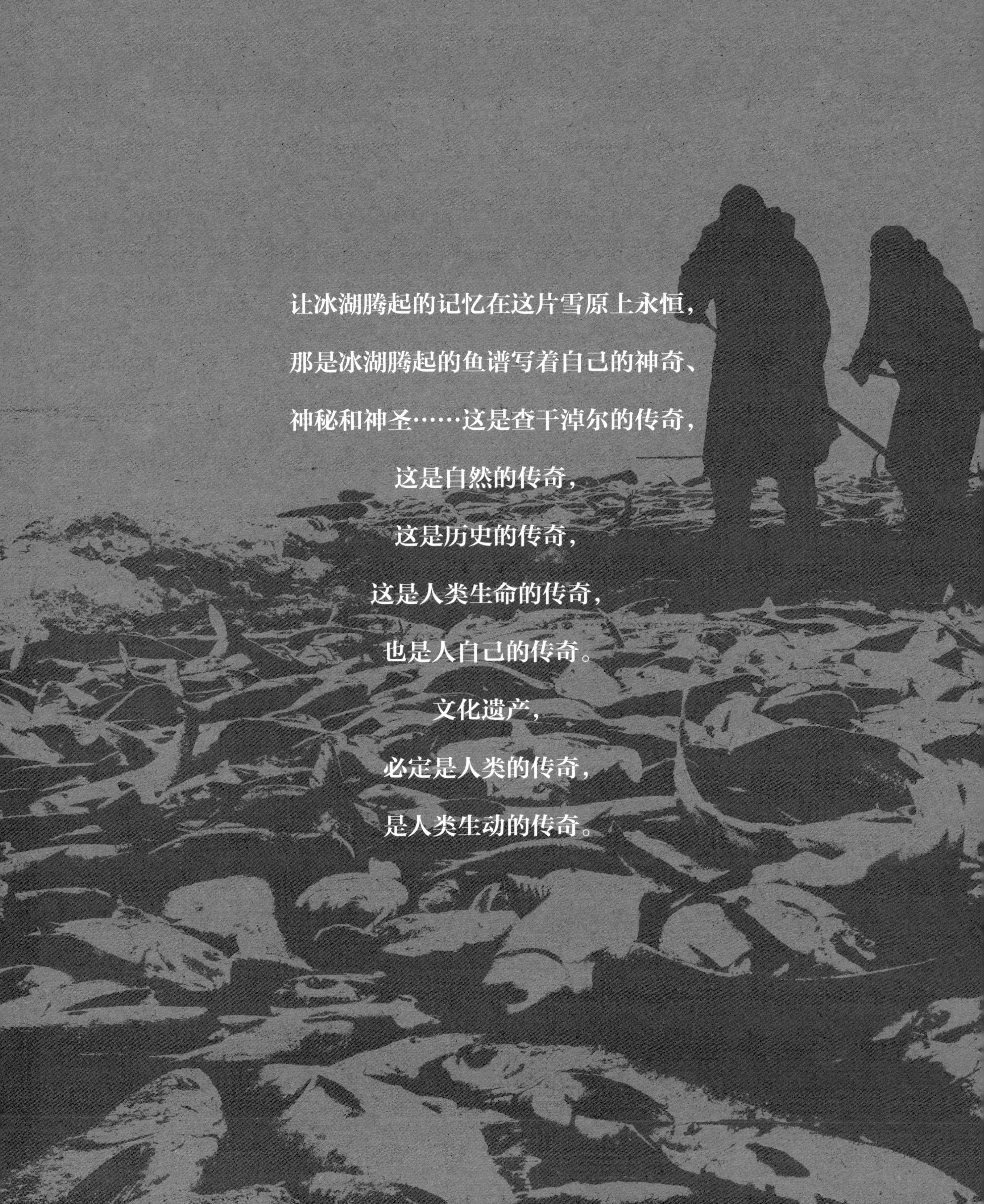

让冰湖腾起的记忆在这片雪原上永恒，
那是冰湖腾起的鱼谱写着自己的神奇、
神秘和神圣……这是查干淖尔的传奇，
这是自然的传奇，
这是历史的传奇，
这是人类生命的传奇，
也是人自己的传奇。
文化遗产，
必定是人类的传奇，
是人类生动的传奇。

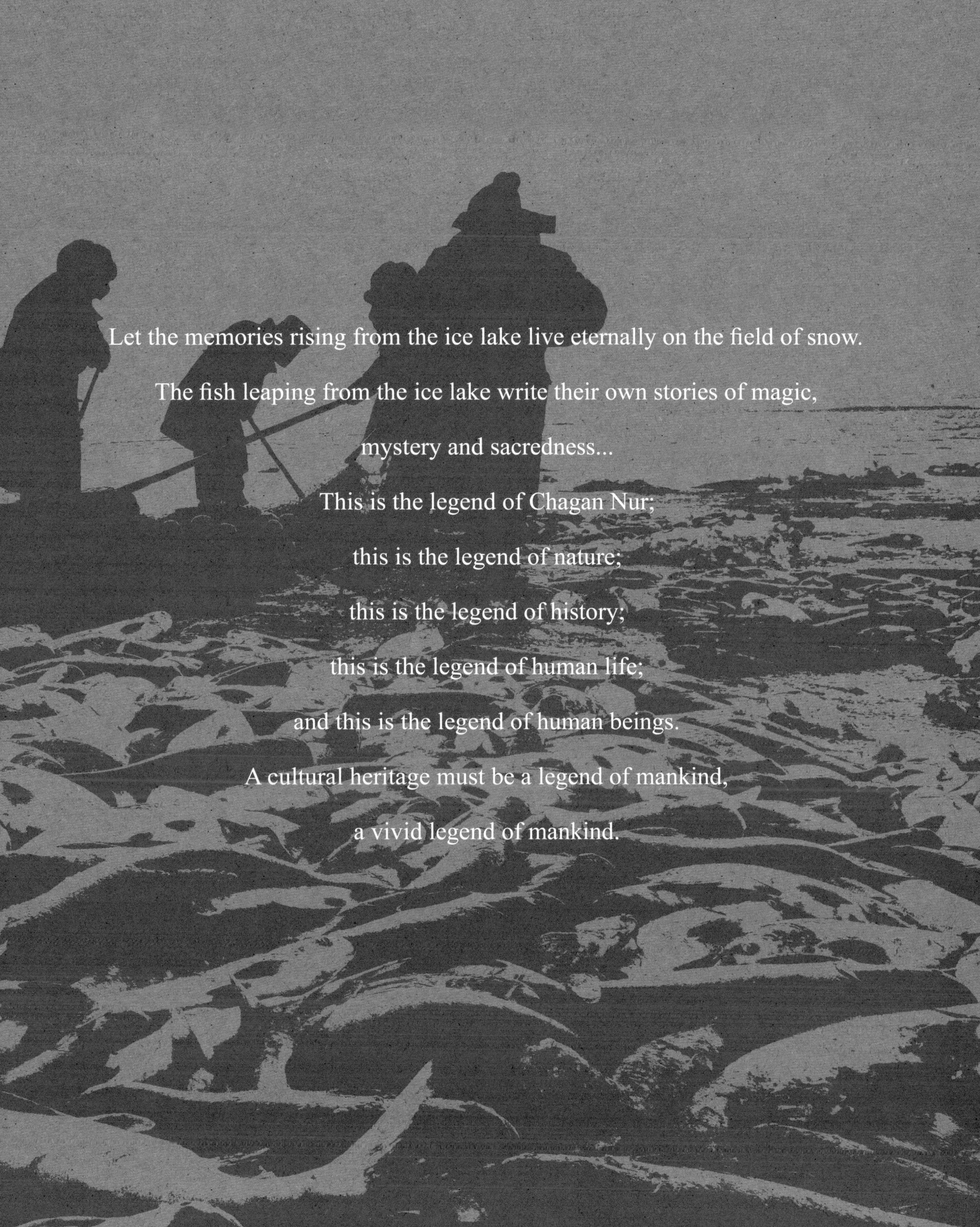
Let the memories rising from the ice lake live eternally on the field of snow.
The fish leaping from the ice lake write their own stories of magic,
mystery and sacredness...
This is the legend of Chagan Nur;
this is the legend of nature;
this is the legend of history;
this is the legend of human life;
and this is the legend of human beings.
A cultural heritage must be a legend of mankind,
a vivid legend of mankind.

老北风，把科尔沁凝固了；炮烟雪，把科尔沁埋住了。科尔沁的湖泊，仿佛消失在地平线的远方。湖泊，人们的向往中始终有它的存在。因为，它总结了大地的优势，它让干燥的草原具有了活态气息……

The old north wind has frozen Horqin; the whirling snow has buried Horqin. The lakes of Horqin seem to have disappeared from the distant horizon. Lakes, people have always yearned for them, for they embody all that is good on the earth and breathe life into the arid grassland...

湖泊以其粗犷豪放和生生不息的性格彰显着它强大的生命力，睁大了它智慧的眼睛。

The lake, with its bold and uninhibited character, manifests its incredible vitality and opens its eye of wisdom.

太阳照在查干冰原上

The Sun Shines on the Chagan Nur Ice Field

摄影 / 刘玉忱
Photograph by / Liu Yuchen

摄影 / 闫来锁
Photograph by / Yan Laisuo

查干淖尔是北方草甸的智慧的眼睛，它日夜在向四野观望。春天的观望是以它枯黄的姿态展现出它的遥远，夏天的观望展现出它的翠绿，秋天的观望展现出它的金黄，冬天的观望展现出它的洁白和圣洁。而洁白就是无瑕，就是永恒，冬天的查干淖尔展现出它无限的永恒。它以自己的永恒捍卫自然和人类的本色。

Chagan Nur is an eye of wisdom on the northern grassland. It gazes at the wilderness around it day and night. In spring, it is a withered yellow that reflects its remoteness; in summer, it is lush green; in autumn, it is golden yellow; and in winter it is pure white and chaste. Pure white is unblemished and eternal. In winter, Chagan Nur reveals that it is eternal. With this eternity, it safeguards nature and human nature.

冬季，当西伯利亚的寒风吹拂着科尔沁，当白雪覆盖了厚厚的荒原，查干淖尔却一下子醒来了。当严寒把冰垒砌成“山”，当凛冽的寒风吹裂了坚冰，当马蹄的铁掌敲击着查干淖尔的冰面，无数的记忆在这里恢复了，无数被忽略的历史在这里生成了，无数被忽略的自然在这里回归了，无数被遗忘的故事在这里跳动了，于是，冰湖腾鱼了……

In winter, when Siberia’s cold wind blows across Horqin, when white snow blankets the wilderness, Chagan Nur suddenly comes to life. When the cold makes mountains of ice, when the chilly wind cracks ice, when horseshoes tap the icy surface of Chagan Nur, countless memories are restored here; countless neglected histories are regenerated here; countless neglected nature return here; countless forgotten stories are revitalized here. And so fish start leaping on the ice lake…

让冰湖腾起的记忆在这片雪原上永恒，那是冰湖腾起的鱼谱写着自己的神奇、神秘和神圣……这是查干淖尔的传奇，这是自然的传奇，这是历史的传奇，这是人类生命的传奇，也是人自己的传奇。文化遗产，必定是人类的传奇，是人类生动的传奇。

Let the memories rising from the ice lake live eternally on the field of snow. The fish leaping from the ice lake write their own stories of magic, mystery and sacredness... This is the legend of Chagan Nur; this is the legend of nature; this is the legend of history; this is the legend of human life; and this is the legend of human beings. A cultural heritage must be a legend of mankind, a vivid legend of mankind.

摄影/闫来锁
Photograph by / Yan Laisuo

北方查干淖尔是一个特定的区域地理概念，从具体方位上看，它位于兴安盟和呼伦贝尔市以南，通辽市以东，肇东湿地平原以西，长白山余脉伊通大黑山以北的广垠范围之内，这里具有自己灿烂的文化内涵，而冬捕渔猎为其重要特征，再有便是地处偏远而荒凉生态之中的自然原色……

Chagan Nur is a geographic region located to the south of Xingan Prefecture and Hulunbeier Prefecture, to the east of Zhelimu Prefecture, to the west of the Zhaodong Wetland Plain, and to the north of the Yitong Dahei Mountain, an extension of the Changbai Mountains. This region has a splendid culture of its own, and winter fishing is one of its defining features, along with an unaltered nature thanks to its location in a remote and desolate environment...

今天的查干淖尔，这里聪明灵气的渔夫，悟出了一个深深的道理“邮鱼”，就是把鱼作为古代的“信件”，以古邮驿方式走入生活，进入社会。查干淖尔创造了独特的“腾鱼”方式，他们让鱼“腾飞”了，而且还是“冰鱼”。

The smart fishermen in today's Chagan Nur came up with the brilliant idea of "mailing fish", introducing the fish into more people's lives and society at large by sending them through the ancient system of postal stations. Chagan Nur created a way to make fish fly, and not just any fish, but ice fish.

摄影 / 闫来锁
Photograph by / Yan Laisuo

摄影 / 包文军
Photograph by / Bao Wenjun

远去的鱼阵

An Endless Procession of Fish.

查干淖尔的邮鱼智慧，创意于第十三届“最后的渔猎部落冰雪文化旅游节”。那次，从遥远的海南岛来了一批客人观赏冰上捕鱼，他们天天在冰上走啊、看哪，跟着渔夫的网看不够，又从冰上抱起一条条大鱼，拍呀！照呀！到头来，只好恋恋不舍地把鱼放在冰上，发出一声叹息。

Chagan Nur’s idea about “mailing fish” originated from the 13th “Festival of Ice and Snow Culture Tourism at the Last Fishing Tribe”. During that event, a group of visitors from the distant island of Hainan came to watch the ice fishing activities. Every day they wandered on the ice, looking at everything. They watched the fishermen working with the net, and picked up a big fish from the ice and took endless photographs. Eventually, they placed the fish back on the ice reluctantly, followed by a deep sigh.

"北鱼虽然好，只是无法到南方啊！"说完，他们就看别的去了。

"The fish in the north are certainly very good, but there is no way to get them in the south!" After this comment, they left to look at something else.

南方人的这句话，让查干淖尔人开始沉思。是啊，查干淖尔的鲜鱼好是好，但是只在北方流通，那是咱查干淖尔的人目光短浅！不行啊，要让带着冰雪味儿的鲜鱼迅速"飞"往南方才行，不能再等了呀！

The southerners' remarks got the people of Chagan Nur thinking. Yes, the Chagan Nur fish are delicious, but they are marketed only in the north, and that is the result of our short-sightedness! No, that won't do. We must let the fresh fish that taste of ice and snow "fly" to the south, and we mustn't wait any longer!

南方客人的感慨，一下子启发了查干淖尔人，要发展查干淖尔渔猎文化，要让鱼"飞"起来，穿越中华九百六十万平方公里的大地，到达中国的千家万户。就在这天夜里，查干淖尔人做出了一个大胆的决定，他们要开创一个冰湖奇迹——邮鱼。让鱼"腾飞"起来，让鱼展翅成为"飞天"。

于是，查干淖千百年的古老"邮路"复活了。
于是，最后的渔猎部落新生了。

立刻，网上“邮鱼”迅速在北方寒冷的冰原上铺开。

The wistful comment of the tourists from the south had inspired the people of Chagan Nur to promote the fishing culture of Chagan Nur, to make the fish “fly” across China’s

9.6 million square kilometers of land to reach millions of households. On that night, the people of Chagan Nur reached a bold decision: They wanted to create a miracle out of the ice lake – to “mail fish”, helping them take off, spread their wings, and fly.

As a result, the postal road used centuries ago in Chagan Nur was resurrected.

As a result, the last fishing tribe was reborn.

Instantly, the business of “mailing fish” took off through the internet and quickly spread on the cold ice fields of the north.

那，也是一张“网”，它一张开，一网“打尽”了中

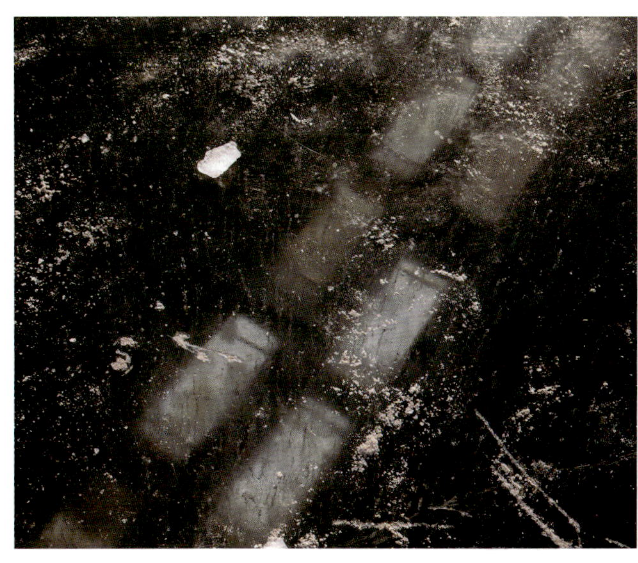

国的千家万户。人们只要想吃查干淖尔鱼的美味、鲜味，在二三天内，冰湖的空中飞鱼可以立刻到达……

查干淖尔的冰鱼，就这样“飞”进了人类现代生活之中，再不只是一个美妙的渔猎文化的传说。

That too was a “net”. It opened up and “caught” thousands of households in China. Delicious Chagan Nur fish can be delivered to anyone who has a craving in a matter of two or three days...

摄影 / 刘玉忱
Photograph by / Liu Yuchen

In this way, the ice fish of Chagan Nur have “flown” into modern life. It is no longer a fishing culture that exists only in legends.

当寒冷把北方大地凝固成冰天雪地，查干淖尔在静静地诉说着自己的故事，那千年的走向今天依然活态的存在。查干淖尔给冰雪文化搭建了一个祭祀自然的平台，诉说传奇的平台，传颂民谣的平台，呼唤祖先的平台……查干淖尔，这是人类发现生命永

摄影 / 刘玉忱
Photograph by / Liu Yuchen

When the cold freezes the northern land into a world of ice and snow, Chagan Nur is quietly telling the story of a thousand-year-old culture that remains vibrant today. Chagan Nur is the only place that has built a platform for worshiping nature, for narrating legends, for singing folk songs, for invoking ancestors… Chagan Nur, it is the coordinates and platform for humans to discover the eternity of life

为了捍卫人类理性的存在，为了捍卫大自然的原本生态，为了捍卫世代传承的美丽和壮观，更是为了探索生命终究是否能够永恒，查干淖尔冰雪文化日夜在坚冰厚雪上下进行、进行……

In order to safeguard the rational existence of human, in order to defend the original ecology of nature, in order to preserve the beauty and magnificence passed down through generations, and in order to explore whether life can be eternal, the culture of ice and snow at Chagan Nur is being lived out day and night on top of and beneath the hard ice and thick snow...

如果你向往人间真正的天堂，那么查干淖尔在这里默默地等你，已经等了数千年了。当渔夫的脚步踏遍了冰雪覆盖的查干淖尔，当渔夫手中的冰镩凿开厚厚的冰层，当冰块闪着七色光芒腾向天空，当冰块落地砸起地上的雪浪，当凛冽的寒风冻裂了渔夫的脸庞，当霜雪凝聚在渔夫的眉毛和胡子上，查干淖尔的强大气场在北方荒野上扩散……

If you yearn for a real paradise on earth, Chagan Nur quietly awaits, as it has for the past thousands of years. When the fishermen's footsteps travel across the snow-covered Chagan Nur, when the chisel in the fishermen's hands cut through the thick layer of ice, when the ice blocks bounce up as they reflect the sunlight, when the ice blocks hit the ground, sending out a rippling wave of snow, when the frigid wind cracks the fishermen's faces, when the frost covers fishermen's eyebrows and beard, the powerful spiritual aura of Chagan Nur is spreading across the wilderness of the north...

岁月不再孤独，大地不再单调，查干淖尔不再孤寂，冰湖不再沉睡，渔猎文化正从远古徐徐地延

摄影 / 闫来锁
Photograph by / Yan Laisuo

续、传承地走来，它留住了久远，它活化了当今，它感染了未来……

查干淖尔在冰雪中诞生，它是严寒冬季的伙伴。严寒没有伙伴就不会洁白，查干淖尔没有冰雪就不会永生。科尔沁把冰雪收入到自己的心底，大地把人类最灿烂的精华——冰雪文化变成世界文化宝库中的瑰宝。

Time is no longer lonely; the land is no longer monotonous; Chagan Nur is no longer alone; the ice lake is no longer slumbering. The fishing culture from ancient times has been inherited and continued. It is eternal, it has enlivened the present, and it will influence the future...

Chagan Nur was born in the ice and snow, and it is a partner of the cold winter. The cold cannot maintain its pure whiteness without a partner, and Chagan Nur will not be eternal without ice and snow. Horqin has wholeheartedly accepted the ice and snow, and developed the culture of ice and snow that is now part of a treasure trove of world cultures.

摄影 / 闫来锁
Photograph by / Yan Laisuo

摄影 / 闫来锁
Photograph by / Yan Laisuo

摄影/闫来锁
Photograph by / Yan Laisuo

每年的查干淖尔冬季都将成为一个盛典。那是留在岁月中的一个刻板，那是刻在人类生命历程上的一个符号，那是一个杰出生命书写出的一部天书。千年的记忆，万载的呼唤，自然的色彩，人类的智慧，一一书写其中。

人类在等待着生命去解读它。

解读查干淖尔成为人类通向理想的生活追求。

Every year, winter will be a festive event in Chagan Nur. It is an engraving board of time, a symbol carved into the history of human progress, and a book without words but written by countless lives. A thousand years of memories, a beckoning from ten thousand years ago, the colors of nature, human wisdom…everything is

Humans are waiting to read and understand this book with their lives.

Understanding Chagan Nur has become a path in the pursuit of an ideal life.

打开这部天书，才能进入解读的时刻。这样的时刻，只有走进查干淖尔，呼吸着查干淖尔的气息，品悟着查干淖尔的记忆，倾听着查干淖尔的诉说，你才能幸福地打开查干淖尔的这部天书。

Only when you open this book can you start to understand. You must go to Chagan Nur, breathe the air of Chagan Nur, appreciate the memories of Chagan Nur, and listen to what Chagan Nur has to say in order to blissfully open this book .

摄影 / 闫来锁
Photograph by / Yan Laisuo

摄影 / 闫来锁
Photograph by / Yan Laisuo

品读查干淖尔，解读查干淖尔，自然在渴望着，历史在等待着，人类在呼唤着，生命在邀请着……

在查干淖尔的传统中，生命与生命时刻在诉说，马是自己的亲兄弟，狼是自己的老朋友，鱼是渔夫的亲生儿女，冰是它们时刻不离手的茶杯，雪是黏豆包的砂糖，霜是豆面卷子的炒面，大绳是渔夫们的腰带，小绳是姑娘们头上的花朵，皮袄是渔夫们火炕上的棉被，窝棚是渔夫们的理想的别墅……

Read Chagan Nur and interpret Chagan Nur. Nature, history, people and life await you there...

In the tradition of Chagan Nur, lives touch lives. To the people there, horses are their brothers, wolves are their old friends, fish are the fishermen's children, ice is the tea cup that never leaves their hand, snow is the sugar in the sticky-bean buns, frost is the fried noodles that go with the bean flour buns, the big braid rope is the fisherman's belt, the small ropes are the flowers in a girl's hair, the sheepskin jackets are the fishermen's quilts on the heated *kang*; the shacks are the fishermen's ideal villas...

摄影 / 刘玉忱
Photograph by / Liu Yuchen

祈盼的时刻
The Moment of Hope and Expectation

查干淖尔啊，你是东北民族的火炕，人们听着二人转，唱着古老的歌谣，在这面火炕上幸福地沉睡成长。

生命和工具都在注视，静止中带有生动的诉说，工具沉睡在冰雪上了吗？人被严寒冻僵了吗？所有的物件都成了生命的原色体。

Oh, Chagan Nur, you are the heated *kang* for the people of Northeast China. People listen to the singing-dancing duet, sing ancient songs, and grow up happily on this heated *kang* on which they slumber.

Life and tools are watching. In stillness there are vivid narratives. Are the tools sleeping soundly on the ice and snow? Are the people frozen by the severe cold? All the objects have taken on the original colors of life.

科尔沁有自己的乐呵时刻，这个时刻，就是“鱼来啦”。鱼，总会来吗？从前有一伙人来到查干淖尔。走时，网房子的主人给他们一人两条鱼，然后问他们：“你们还来不来啦？”一个人要了人家的东西，还来吗？再来的话，不是还来要“东西”吗？于是，他们在沉思，怎么回答呢？他们在沉思。渔民也在沉思。突然，人们悟出了道理，他们大声回答道：“还来——！还来——！”

Horqin has its moment of joy. That moment is when the fish come. Will the fish always come? Once upon a time a group of people visited Chagan Nur. When they left, the owner of the net shed gave two fish to each of them, and then asked, “Will you come again?” How can anybody come back again after accepting a gift ? If you do, wouldn’t you be coming back to receive more gifts? So they started to ponder: How should we reply? As they pondered, the fisherman also pondered. All of a sudden, they realized the truth, and together they replied loudly: “Yes, we will come again!”

摄影/闫来锁
Photograph by / Yan Laisuo

在那遥远的地方
In a Faraway Place

于是，渔夫乐了。

是啊，渔夫们在等待，如果你回答“不来了”，渔夫们就会追你去，撵出二里地也会把给你的鱼要回来。因为，他们给你的是“鱼”，但等你回答的却是“希望。”

如果你回答“不来了”，渔夫们还打啥？

相遇查干淖尔

An Encounter with Chagan Nur

摄影 / 闫来锁

Photograph by / Yan Laisuo

摄影/闫来锁
Photograph by / Yan Laisuo

一种古老的民俗，在科尔沁的查干淖尔，已深深的印入人类的心灵。

你要记住它，你要读懂它，你要品悟它，你要传承它，你要保护它，你要跟随它，你要走进它……

它，是一处深深的走向，久远的走向。

查干淖尔，是一个令人惊喜不断的地方。

This made the fisherman happy.

Yes. The fisherman was waiting. If your answer to the question was “no”, the fisherman would chase you and take back the fish, because he gave you fish but expected your answer to be “hope”. If your answer was “no”, what could the fisherman hope to catch?

An ancient custom in Chagan Nur of Horqin has been deeply imprinted in people’s minds.

You have to remember it. You have to read and understand it. You have to appreciate it. You have to carry it forward. You have to protect it. You have to follow it. You have to enter it…

It is a place with depth and history.

Chagan Nur is a place that constantly surprises.

摄影 / 闫来锁
Photograph by / Yan Laisuo

马轮子拉出的巨网在冰面上垒起的鱼垛，鱼垛抵挡着北方平原的冰雪寒风，丰收畅想了渔夫的理想。当冰层断裂的巨响骤然升起，那是鱼垛压裂了冰层。当爬犁拖鱼而归，冰院子里堆起了鱼山；当鱼墙照亮了雪原，把黄昏的灿烂凝固在夕阳中，查干淖尔活起来了。

The net dragged out by the horse winch leaves stacks of fish on the ice. The fish stacks withstand the ice, snow and cold winds of the northern plains. The good harvest bolsters the fishermen's dreams. When the ice ruptures and sends out a deafening noise, it is because the weight of the fish stacks has fractured the ice layer. When the sledge returns with the catch, a fish mountain rises in the ice yard. When the fish wall illuminates the snow field and the brilliance of the fading day is captured by the sunset, Chagan Nur comes alive.

似乎地球上的每一个人的血脉和血液里，都有一个意识在流淌，保护它，我们的查干淖尔；留住它，人类的查干淖尔……

也许，正是因为这种意识，人类才能跨越千年，自然才能停留千年，现实才能留住活态，未来才能保住有滋有味，青山绿水才是我们的乡愁。在这里，人类表现出前所未有的辉煌与淡定……

It seems that a thought courses through the blood of everyone on earth: Protect it, our Chagan Nur; preserve it, the Chagan Nur that belongs to all mankind...

Perhaps it is because of this awareness that human history can span millennia; that nature can be preserved for thousands of years; that the present is alive; that the future is still palatable; and that it is green mountains and clear waters that make us nostalgic. Here, mankind has shown unprecedented glory and serenity...

一瞬间，萨满博的英魂升腾在万年的青山头，披着白雪的敖包，正在倾声吟唱着与自然的相会，与历史的诉说，与生活的触摸，与未来的衔接……

Instantly, Shaman Bo's soul rises up to the age-old Qingshantou; the snow-covered *aobao* (sacred stone heap) is singing a song about its encounter with nature, its dialogue with history, its contact with life, its connection with the future…

这时候，我们每一个人都会感觉到查干淖尔从容诉说历史的功能，那是因为冰雪陪伴着生命，冰雪已替换成金山银山。

冰湖

In such moments, we all experience how Chagan Nur is capable of placidly narrating history, for it is ice and snow that accompany life. The ice and snow have been replaced by mountains of gold and silver.

一壶老酒雪上醇香，两碗饺子冰原飘荡。古往今来，哪里是生命的天堂，查干淖尔——渔猎文化的故乡。丰收时刻的马蹄踏着冰雪，夜班归来的渔夫，已成了冰人，雪物。新年的钟声依然敲响，所有的年节都融入在渔猎的梦乡，丰收的喜悦谱写了千年的冰雪辉煌。查干淖尔，一个人类爱不够的地方。一个人不能不去的地方。一起去到达这个心灵时刻想回归的去处，与冰雪的鱼儿做伴娱乐的天堂。

A pot of liquor becomes mellower with snow. Two bowls of dumplings float on the ice field. Throughout the ages, where is the paradise of life? Chagan Nur – home of the fishing culture. At harvest time, horses gallop on the ice and snow. The fishermen returning from their night shift have become men of ice and objects of snow. The

鱼，在冰湖水浪中沉沦，却是等待着腾升
Surging Fish in the Icy Lake

摄影 / 刘玉忱
Photograph by / Liu Yuchen

New Year's bell is still tolling, and all the holidays and festivities have blended into the land of fishing. The joy of a good harvest has written brilliant chapters in ice and snow for a thousand years. Chagan Nur—a place beloved by people and where you must visit once. Let us go together to the place our hearts yearn to return, the paradise where the fish of ice and snow are our partners in joyful times.

查干淖尔它把人类热爱它的生命轻轻托起，又轻轻地放下；它小心地举起，又虔诚地摆放，让无数的历史和自然在岁月的星空飞溅，它让人类之爱和冰湖一起腾飞，查干淖尔就这样凝固在人类岁月的刻板上。

Chagan Nur has softly lifted the human lives that love it and gently put it down. It holds it up carefully and places it down devoutly, so that countless histories and nature splash and scatter in the starry sky of time. It allows human love to take flight with the ice lake. Chagan Nur is thus solidified on the engraving plate of human history.

保留查干湖文化遗产
献给人类《冰湖腾鱼》
PRESERVING THE CULTURAL HERITAGE OF THE CHAGAN LAKE *FISHING ON THE ICE*: A GIFT TO ALL

撰文 / 闫来锁

By / Yan Laisuo

我在查干湖工作了30年，这里是我的第二故乡。我深深地热爱着这个地方，这些年来，在渔业生产、品牌建设、旅游开发、生态保护以及文化传承等方面做了一些具体工作。查干湖冰雪渔猎文化旅游节已经成功举办了14届，进一步通过各类媒体和宣传平台扩大宣传，将查干湖文化推向世界，打好“绿水青山就是金山银山，冰天雪地也是金山银山”生态品牌，做大做强冰雪渔猎文化旅游产业，保护和传承查干湖渔猎文化是我的一份责任。

I have spent 30 years working at Chagan Lake, which has become my second hometown. I have a profound love for this place. Over the years, I have been able to achieve some concrete results for this place in terms of fishing production, branding, tourism development, ecological protection and cultural preservation. The Chagan Lake Ice and Snow Fishing and Hunting Culture Tourism Festival has been successfully held for 14 years. Going forward, the Chagan Lake culture will be even more extensively promoted through a variety of media and publicity platforms to introduced it to the world. We will further develop the tourism industry around the ice and snow fishing culture by building an ecological brand with the belief that "Clear waters and green mountains are gold mountains and silver mountains, and so are the ice and snow." I deem it my responsibility to ensure the protection and continuation of the Chagan Lake fishing culture.

编辑出版一部具有权威性和文献价值的文学影像读物正是时候，如何推进？我想只有特别了解查干湖历史以及民俗文化的专家和具有国际水准的摄影家才能完成。

I believe it is necessary to produce and publish a literary and photographic coverage of Chagan Lake that is authoritative and has documentary value. But how to go about doing this? It seems to me that the task can only be successfully carried out by an expert with a special understanding of the history and folk culture of Chagan Lake and a photographer of international repute.

思来想去，两个人浮现在我的脑海。一位是曹保明先生，另一位是摄影家边缘先生。

曹保明先生是中国著名文化学者。他 30 年来坚持深入吉林各地挖掘整理当地的民族、民俗、民间文化，我在查干湖工作了 30 年，与曹保明先生也相识 30 年。记得 20 世纪 90 年代初，曹先生来查干湖需要从省城坐火车到塔虎城小站，我们用马车去接他。

自从举办了渔猎文化节，我年年邀请他，他已经几乎成了我们“最后的渔猎部落”的一个“部落”成员了。

他撰写的《最后的渔猎部落》一书由上海文化出版社出版发行，立刻在国内外产生了重要影响，并荣获“徐霞客杯”散文著作大奖。

闫来锁 / 曹保明
Yan Laisuo / Cao Baoming

As I pondered the question, two people came to my mind. One is Mr. Cao Baoming, and the other is the photographer Bian Yuan.

Mr. Cao Baoming is a well-known scholar of Chinese culture. Over the past 30 years, he has persisted in traveling all around Jilin to discover and compile local ethnic and folk cultures. I have worked in the Chagan Lake for 30 years and have known Mr. Cao Baoming for as long. I remember picking him up with a horse-drawn carriage in the early 1990s at the train station of small-town Tahucheng, where he had traveled by train from the provincial capital to visit Chagan Lake.

Since the debut of the fishing and hunting festival, I have invited him to it every year, and he has almost become a member of our "last hunting and fishing tribe".

His book, *The Last Fishing and Hunting Tribe* published by the Shanghai Cultural Publishing House, was immediately influential both at home and abroad, and received the grand prize for prose writing from the "Xu Xiake Cup" awards.

中国民间文艺家协会主席冯骥才先生做客中央电视台时，曾介绍过他，说："每逢年节，合家团聚，我知道有一个人却在路上，他就是曹保明，中国东北的许多文化是被他抢救，保护下来的。"

边缘先生是一位行走世界的自然地理摄影师，有着中国国家级媒体编采经验，摄影艺术造诣得到中国权威机构和世界环保组织的肯定。

一次偶遇，我与边缘先生结下了深厚的"查干湖"情缘。记得那是 2006 年 10 月初的一个清晨，我在湖畔检查工作时，发现一个人神情专注地举着相机在拍鸟，观其举止与众不同，引起了我的关注。

In a CCTV interview, Mr. Feng Jicai, Chairman of the Association of China Folk Literature and Art Association, described Mr. Cao Baoming with these remarks, "Each year during Chinese New Year, a time for family reunions, I know one person is still on the road, and that person is Cao Baoming, who has salvaged and protected many cultures of Northeast China."

Mr. Bian Yuan is a globe-trotting photographer of natural geography. He has editing and reporting experience at the national media level, and his photographic art has been recognized by official Chinese institutions and international environmental protection organizations.

A chance encounter at the Chagan Lake marked the beginning of my friendship with Mr. Bian Yuan. It was on a morning in early October of 2006. I was inspecting some work around the lake when I saw a person taking photographs of birds with a look of intense focus on his face. His demeanor stood out from everyone else and attracted my attention.

交流中得知，边缘先生是追踪白鹤迁徙途经查干湖，他觉得这么大的水域，生态保护得如此之好，一定会吸引众多鸟类在此安家落户，也一定是鸟类迁徙的驿站。

边缘行摄世界各地，追踪鸟类迁徙 26 年，来查干湖还是第一次，我向边缘先生详细介绍了查干湖的历史、人文、生态、自然及冬捕的神奇与壮观，听后他欣然决定安排档期拍摄冬捕。

边缘先生如约而至，从此开始用摄影家独特的视角记录查干湖渔猎，转眼拍摄了 10 年。

As we talked, I learned that Mr. Bian Yuan had followed the migrating white cranes to Chagan Lake. He felt that such a large body of water, with its ecology so well preserved, would surely attract all kinds of birds to settle here, and was sure to be a rest stop for migrating birds.

Bian Yuan had been photographing around the world and following migratory birds for 26 years, but it was his first trip to Chagan Lake. So I told him all about the history, culture, ecology, nature and the magical and spectacular winter fishing of Chagan Lake. He gladly decided to schedule some time for photographing the winter fishing event.

Later, he returned as promised. Ten years have passed since then, throughout which time he has used a photographer's unique perspective to document the fishing activities on Chagan Lake.

编纂《冰湖腾鱼》这部反映中国冰雪文化遗产的经典读本恰逢其时，十分必要。作者对查干湖有一种难以割舍的情怀，将“冰湖腾鱼”精彩动人的瞬间和过程倾注在了笔端和镜头，展示给了读者。

《冰湖腾鱼》是一部重要的地域文献，是一个历史的文本。在这部著作中，他们把查干湖的文化进行了全方位的归纳和整体的概括。在这里，他们用切实的文笔和精准的镜头，全景记录和检验了查干湖人的生活，保留了查干湖这优秀的人间遗产，献给人类一部珍贵的《冰湖腾鱼》，让我心中充满了感动。

The compilation and publication of this book, a classic reader on the Chinese ice and snow heritage, is both timely and necessary. The authors care deeply about the Chagan Lake, and with their writing and photography, they have captured the exciting and moving moments in ice fishing for the readers.

Ice Lake · Leaping Fish is an important record of a region and a historical text. In this book, the authors have attempted an exhaustive and comprehensive look at the culture of Chagan Lake. Through accurate written accounts and a sharp lens, they offer us a panoramic record and examination of the lives of the people of Chagan Lake. They have preserved the outstanding human heritage of Chagan Lake and given us this invaluable book. I am deeply touched by what they have accomplished.

在冰雪文化遗产概念这个领域，迄今为止很少有一个地域如查干湖一样的渔猎文化，已反复地经过人类的检验。接受这个检验，就成了查干湖主动迎接人类文明的姿态，让严谨的科学尺度在这里衡量它。遗产终究要受到人类思想尺度的衡量。

2008 年，当国内的专家、联合国教科文组织的专家衡量查干湖冬捕文化时，所有评委一致为这片土地投了赞成票，将查干湖“冰湖腾鱼”评为“吉林八景”之一，对千百年来生活在这里的人们对自己文化的坚守给出了一个满意的答案。

In the field of snow and ice cultural heritage, few fishing cultures have been tested repeatedly by humans like the one at Chagan Lake. Accepting this test is a demonstration of Chagan Lake's willingness to embrace human civilizations and to be examined by rigorous scientific standards. After all, human heritages will always have to be measured by the dimensions of human thoughts.

In 2008, when experts from China and UNESCO reviewed the Chagan Lake winter fishing culture, the members of the evaluation committee voted unanimously in favor of Changan Lake, designating the ice fishing here as one of the "Eight Sights of Jilin", a welcome recognition of the people here who have adhered to their culture for thousands of years.

查干湖里，最出名的就是“胖头鱼”，辽代的长春州（塔虎城，塔虎即“胖头鱼”之意）就以此命名。2001 年这里的代表性符号“胖头鱼”获得中国绿色食品发展中心绿色食品认证；而后自 2003 年起连续 14 年获得 “有机食品”认证。2006 年 10 月，查干湖鱼荣获农业部颁发的中国名牌农产品称号。

中央电视台经典纪录片《舌尖上的中国》第一集中就有对查干湖冬捕及查干湖全鱼宴的报道。查干湖鱼多年来享誉中外，堪称中国淡水鱼第一品牌，是国人餐桌上的首选美味，查干湖成为人们向往的冬季冰雪旅游之地。

The most famous fish in Chagan Lake is the *pangtou* fish (bighead carp). The Changchun Prefecture in the Liao Dynasty was named for it. (The prefecture was named Tahu Town back then; “tahu” means *pangtou* fish.) In 2001, the *pangtou* fish logo for Chagan Lake received the certification of green food from the China Green Food Development Center, and for 14 consecutive years since 2003, it has been certified as organic food. In October 2006, Chagan Lake fish was awarded the title of China’s Famous Brand Agricultural Products awarded by the Ministry of Agriculture.

In CCTV’s classic documentary series, “A Bite of China”, the very first episode featured the winter fishing and all-fish feast of Chagan Lake. The fish from Chagan Lake have enjoyed widespread fame both at home and abroad for years. They are arguably the No. 1 brand for freshwater fish in China and are favorite dishes on the dining table. In addition, Chagan Lake has become one of the most popular destinations for winter snow and ice tourism.

这里的鱼类资源非常丰富，曾经以冬捕单网产量 10.45 万公斤和 16.8 万公斤成功创造并打破吉尼斯世界纪录。查干湖冬捕目前已被列为国家级非物质文化遗产。2012 年，查干湖牌注册商标被国家工商行政管理总局认定为中国驰名商标。

There is a wealth of fish resources here. During one winter fishing, Chagan Lake set a new Guinness World Record and then broke that record with single-net catches of 104,500 kilograms and 168,000 kilograms. The Chagan Lake winter fishing has now been designated as a national intangible cultural heritage. In 2012, the registered trademark of the Chagan Lake Brand was recognized by the State Administration for Industry and Commerce as a well-known trademark in China.

十几年来，查干湖渔猎文化在央视新闻频道、综合频道、中文国际频道、少儿频道、旅游频道、财经频道、英语频道、农业频道及各地方台和国际媒体的关心和强力助推下，已被逐步赋予“神奇的查干湖”“四季的查干湖”“世界的查干湖”等诸多内涵。

Over more than a decade, the Chagan Lake fishing culture has been covered by the CCTV News Channel, Integrated Channel, Chinese International Channel, Children's Channels, Travel Channels, Financial Channel, English Channel and Agricultural Channels, and by various local and international media. Thanks to their attention and vigorous promotion, Chagan Lake has gradually come to be known as the "magical Chagan Lake", "Chagan Lake for all seasons", and "Chagan Lake of the world".

我们对渔猎文化多年来的坚守和传承，成就了《冰湖腾鱼》这部精彩文字和图片视觉文化并存的文本，这是一部人类生命文化的纪实读本。它翔实而丰满地记录了查干湖文化的充实与饱满，足以打动读者心灵的某一个角落。

Our adherence to and preservation of the fishing culture over the years are what have made this book possible. It is a work that combines wonderful texts and images, as well as a faithful record of human life and culture. It contains informative and exhaustive records of the rich and substantial culture of Chagan Lake, and will strike a chord somewhere in the heart of every reader.

与其说《冰湖腾鱼》是以中国北方民族生活、思想、精神、制度、天文、地理、河流、湖泊、民间、圣贤、古籍、乡土志乃至于民俗等等诸多方面知识来组合并进行梳理与思考的话，不如说《冰湖腾鱼》其实是对本土生活的经验概括，最终使《冰湖腾鱼》成为人与自然和谐的典范。人们爱它的原因是它集中了对这里生活的爱，生命的爱，这会使人类的爱成为一面镜子，人类都可以在其中照见自己，发现自己，这样查干湖才成为真正的人类文化遗产了。

Instead of describing this book as a comprehensive contemplation of the Chagan Lake culture that draws on knowledge about the life, thought, spirituality, systems, astronomy, geography, rivers, lakes, folklores, sages, ancient texts, local annals and folk customs of the people of China's northern reaches, it would be better to say that the book is a summary of the local life experience, and ultimately offers a model of how man and nature can live in harmony. This place is beloved because it demonstrates such a love of life, which becomes a mirror in which humans can see themselves and find themselves. In this way, Chagan Lake will truly be a cultural heritage shared by all.

在编纂此文本的日子里，包文军、杨萌，以及王文彦、单军国、张文平、王耀臣、李凌昊等共同参与了文字材料的提供、校对和图片的整理。

During the compilation of this text, Bao Wenjun, Yang Meng, Wang Wenyan, Shan Junguo, Zhang Wenping, Wang Yaochen, Li Linghao and others contributed by providing written materials and assistance in proofreading and picture collating.

（本文作者系吉林省查干湖国家级自然保护管理局负责人闫来锁先生）

(Yan Laisuo is Director of the Jilin Province Chagan Lake National Nature Conservation Authority.)

图书在版编目（CIP）数据

冰湖腾鱼：查干湖最后的渔猎部落 / 边缘著、摄影．
-- 北京：五洲传播出版社，2016.11
ISBN 978-7-5085-3271-4

Ⅰ．①冰… Ⅱ．①边… Ⅲ．①蒙古族 — 捕捞 — 民族文化 — 中国 — 摄影集②蒙古族 — 渔猎 — 民族文化 — 中国 — 摄影集
Ⅳ．① K281.2-64

中国版本图书馆 CIP 数据核字 (2016) 第 254940 号

冰湖腾鱼

查干湖最后的渔猎部落

著　　者：边　缘
翻　　译：孙利民
出 版 人：荆孝敏
总 策 划：李永适
责任编辑：王　莉
撰　　文：曹保明　高材林　闫来锁
摄　　影：边　缘　刘玉忱　闫来锁　包文军　张军
装帧设计：深圳雅昌设计中心　大连边缘摄影艺术中心
出版发行：五洲传播出版社
地　　址：北京市海淀区北三环中路 31 号生产力大楼 B 座 6 层
邮　　编：100088
发行电话：010-82005927，010-82007837
网　　址：http://www.cicc.org.cn，http://www.thatsbooks.com
印　　刷：雅昌文化（集团）有限公司
版　　次：2017 年 1 月第 1 版第 1 次印刷
开　　本：16 开
印　　张：19
字　　数：39 千字
定　　价：390.00 元

美国国家地理学会是世界上最大的非营利科学与教育组织之一。学会成立于 1888 年，以“增进与普及地理知识”为宗旨，致力于启发人们对地球的关心。美国国家地理学会通过杂志、电视节目、影片、音乐、电台、图书、DVD、地图、展览、活动、学校出版计划、交互式媒体与商品来呈现世界。美国国家地理学会的会刊《国家地理》杂志，以英文及其他 33 种语言发行，每月有 3800 万读者阅读。美国国家地理频道在 166 个国家和地区以 34 种语言播放，有 3.2 亿个家庭收看。美国国家地理学会资助超过 10 000 项科学研究、环境保护与探索计划，并支持一项扫除“地理文盲”的教育计划。